MW01274645

Faded Memories – Unleashed

JERRIE CANADY STEWART

outskirtspress

DENVER, COLORADO

Outskirts Press, Inc.
http://www.outskirtspress.com

ISBN: 978-1-4787-6099-3

Outskirts Press and the "OP" logo are trademarks belonging to Outskirts Press, Inc.

PRINTED IN THE UNITED STATES OF AMERICA

CONTENTS

FOREWORD

WE ARE ALL our own identity and are responsible for the choices we make in life.

It's upsetting for me to hear others complain of having had such a hard life or that their parents were divorced or alcoholics and abusive, blaming those circumstances for why they have failed or who they have become.

I don't blame my parents for the choices I have made because I think that all my experiences have made me a stronger person. Heaven knows, I have made some bad choices in my life, but with my faith I have managed to overcome most of them.

The orphanage taught me religion, responsibility, character, faith, etiquette, and social graces; it also provided me with my education, love, caring, food, clothing, and shelter. Should I and my brothers and sisters not have had the opportunity to grow up at the Mills Home Baptist Orphanage, I can't imagine how we would have turned out.

I am at peace with my life today, in my golden years, and look back with pride on my past and from whence I came.

I have been fortunate not to have let my childhood hold me back, but have been able to keep looking forward and looking for the good and purpose in life. I have come to realize that everything that happens to us in life happens for a reason, and only God knows the reasons behind it!

My brothers and sisters have had to endure these times along with me, and I appreciate them so much for it. They may have a different outlook on our early childhood, but these are my own memories and feelings that I have carried throughout my life.

Writing this book has been therapy for me and I am happy to share my experiences with you and hope it will help to assure you that, just because your childhood may not have been a fairy tale, you still have the opportunity to have a fairy-tale ending.

I wish to thank my cousin, Jimmy Canady, for providing the photos of the Canady family.

DEDICATION

THIS BOOK IS dedicated to the memory of my mama, daddy and my sister, Jo, and my four remaining sisters and brothers whom I love dearly. I appreciate them for sharing most of these childhood memories along the way with me.

I also dedicate this book to my three children and hope they will have a better understanding of the experiences their mother has endured, and what has helped to form and make her who she is today. I hope they also realize that I may not have been the "perfect" mother, but that I have tried hard to be. My children and grandchildren are the light of my world!

Looking back, I've tried to understand better the meaning of "home," and those we call "family," and knowing that, "what doesn't kill us, makes us stronger."

My children will come to learn, after raising their own, that no person or book can make you a "perfect" parent or a "perfect" child, but you can enjoy the "perfect" moments along the way. My hope is that they will come to know that there are no two children alike in this world, and that they, too, are their own identity. They and only they are responsible for their actions and the decisions they make throughout their life.

While listening to other kids at the orphanage repeat their childhood memories, it only reminded me that things could always be worse. Nearly three-quarters of them had been abandoned and had faced extreme poverty, and half had been sexually abused. Far too many had been rescued from traumas caused by serial foster-care placements. But you would never know by watching the children at play. Mills Home has saved hundreds of kids from their distressed lives.

I feel that I have battled my bleeding heart for my entire life, trying to touch my emotions, delve into them, experience them, and move forward. I am learning to keep myself protected while I remain exposed and empathetic without being untrusting and guarded. I have been unable to open my heart to people around me because of being susceptible to pain. I've learned that when I remove the shield, I become vulnerable and that can hurt.

Affection is the number one source that makes me feel safe. I never felt I could handle or deserved the love that someone had to give me. It took a lot of sensitivity and patience for those who could break my barrier. Down deep, I always craved love and strived to be loved, like everyone else. I feel I was put here on earth to love completely.

I believe that if we had thrown all our problems in one large pile, after seeing others' problems, we would be picking ours back out.

There were other children in the orphanage that had a much tougher childhood than me and they have achieved a great deal. There are others who have never been able to escape their faded memories.

CHAPTER 1

I WAS BORN in the small town of Wilson, North Carolina, located just on the outskirts of Raleigh.

Born into the family of Herman and Hazel Canady, on a cold, windy morning of March 14, 1943; they named me, simply, Geraldine, with no middle name. I have always been known as "Jerrie." Mama named me after the nurse who tended to her while she was in the Wilson Memorial Hospital, giving birth to me.

(Daddy)   *(Mama)*

My three older sisters—Reba Josephine (Jo), Alice Faye, and Patricia Ann (Pat)—waited anxiously to see their new baby sister arrive home from the hospital. They've always told me that I had lots of black hair and big dark eyes and looked like a little Indian baby. They said that I was sucking on my mama's tit when they first saw me and all they could see was my long black hair and dark eyes.

(House we lived in when I was born in Wilson, N.C. [Then and Now])

Our family lived in the upstairs unit on the right side. Shown in the photo are Jo, Aunt Johnnie (Mama's sister), and Alice Faye. This home has since been restored and has become one of many historical homes in Wilson. I, being the fourth of four girls, have two younger brothers: Sonny Boy and Robert Lee. Our mama had had two miscarriages and six children by the time she turned twenty three years of age.

-Herman Ray Canady and Hazel Estelle Jordan-

The following article was written by a social worker in 1952, stating what Daddy had relayed to them. This may help in understanding my mama and daddy and who they were.

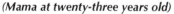

(Mama at twenty-three years old)   *(Daddy in the army [1942])*

"Mr. Canady was able to tell me that he and his wife, Hazel Jordan, lived on adjoining farms in 1937. She was almost sixteen years old when she became pregnant. There seemed to be no doubt in Mr. Canady's mind as to who the father of this child was in that he said, 'I know she is my baby, because she looks just like me.' He went on to say, without encouragement from me, that he knew she had had sexual relations before engaging in such with him. He stated he asked her about this and she said, 'I done this to myself.'

After he was forced by her daddy to marry her, he stated that they lived with his parents for about six months and then moved to a farm near Clayton. They were on this farm for one year and then moved to Wilson. They lived in Wilson until 1945. During that time, he worked in Goldsboro for about two years as a barber, commuting from Wilson. He then worked for a short time at Seymour Johnson Air Base and later for about seventeen months at Stallings Field in Kinston as a barber. He was then called into the army. About three weeks before his induction into the army, he and his wife moved to Raleigh.

Mr. Canady stated that it was while they were living in Wilson, and he working in Goldsboro, that his wife began to drink. She became associated with a woman of questionable reputation, and according to Mr. Canady, his wife began drinking with this woman. He stated this was during the war, when liquor was hard to get. They, therefore, largely drank beer and gin. He questioned his wife about her association with this woman and pleaded with her to stop drinking, but to no avail.

Mr. Canady, at this point, interrupted himself to say to the worker that if he said anything that was wrong that he did not mean to do so but it was because he had only a fifth grade education and did not know how to express himself. Worker assured him that he understood and encouraged him to express himself in those terms and in the manner that meant most to him and would be easiest for him to relate in. During the course of the conversation it was necessary for Mr. Canady to make this same explanation on several occasions. Mr. Canady seemed to feel it was necessary to tell the worker the details of many of his marital experiences and used those terms commonly *used by those not familiar with the scientific or more sociably accept-able terms.*

At this point, Mr. Canady said that he had never been able to fully satisfy his wife in their sexual relationship, and while they were living in Wilson this became more a serious problem. He stated that his wife demanded an intimate relationship every day when once or twice weekly would have sufficed for him. This incompatibility in this phase of their relationship led to complications in their total relationship."

CHAPTER 2

DADDY'S FAMILY'S NAME was "Canady," of German/Scottish descent. The Canady family never accepted my mama's family. You most likely could associate these two families with the Hatfields and McCoys.

The Canady family was a prominent family from Clayton, North Carolina. This family consisted of business men/owners and farmers. Herman was the rowdiest of all the seven Canady boys and he was always known as the "bad boy" of the family. Most of the other members of the family were church goers and seemed to abide by the rules of society.

We called our Canady grandparents "Granny Cora" and "Grandpa Canady" (Arthur and Cora). They had eleven children that consisted of seven boys and four girls: Ralph, Battle, Winston, Gene, Ruffin, Herman and Paul, Lela, Cora Lee, Alene, and Rochelle.

(Grandpa Canady and Granny Cora)

(Uncle Winston)   (Aunt Alene)   (Uncle Paul)

(Uncle Ruffin)   (Aunt Cora Lee)   (Aunt Lela)

(Uncle Gene)   (Aunt Rochelle)   (Herman (daddy

(Uncle Battle)   (Uncle Ralph)

Grandpa Canady and Granny Cora were churchgoers and grand-pa served in every capacity at the church.

Granny Cora was a short, rounded, stout lady who would sit by the stove and spit her snuff into a spittoon by her chair. She was outspoken and didn't hesitate to speak terrible things about the Jordan family when she had the opportunity to do so. We never heard why she seemed to dislike the Jordan family so much. Granny Cora may have felt that mama was the cause of daddy drinking so much or maybe she just felt the Canady family was superior to the Jordan family. Our daddy could do no harm in her eyes. She would never believe that maybe it could have been his own fault for his failures in life.

Every Sunday, the entire Canady family would come together in Granny Cora's living room/bedroom area and sit around the stove and talk for hours.

(Typical Sunday afternoon)

Both of them would always be in their rocking chairs. Of course, Granny Cora's spittoon would be close by.

Granny Cora always had food on the table (covered with a tablecloth) and food was always available for her guests. She would never begin eating until everyone else had filled his or her own plate. To this day, that's a lesson I've carried on with my family.

She was born on July Fourth. Still, every year, there is a big celebration at the Baptist church for Granny Cora, remembering her on her special day. Even though my family always referred to her as Granny Cora, her children referred to her as "Mammy."

(Gathering at the church for Granny Cora's birthday)

CHAPTER 3

MAMA'S MAIDEN NAME was "Jordan," being of Cherokee/Irish descent. The family members were mostly farmers. The three boys were known as being rowdy and womanizers. Their names were Buddy, Ruffin, and Charlie. The six girls were known as "the Jordan girls." They were all beautiful girls: Billie, Lola, Mae, Alma, Hazel, and Virginia (Johnnie). They were all well known in Selma and Smithfield, North Carolina.

We called the Jordan grandparents "Granny Jordan" and "Grandpa Jordan" (John and Percy). Granny Jordan was a large frame woman and she could give you some looks that said, "You better watch out!" She was our storyteller, and when she disciplined us, it was with a switch. She would make us go out and break off our own switch from a nearby bush when we got a "switching" from her.

Grandpa Jordan was a tall, thin man of Cherokee decent. He had only one eye that would ooze. He had lost an eye by accidentally getting poison in it. He chewed tobacco, and he always seemed to have tobacco running out of the corners of his mouth. He did his share of drinking alcohol, too. I was always a little afraid of him as a child. I never really got close to him, so I don't remember a lot about my Grandpa Jordan.

(Granny and Grandpa Jordan)

We spent a lot of time with our Granny Jordan and our aunts and uncles; I remember the special times we had together.

Aunt Billie was a prostitute, and as a matter of fact, that is where she met her husband, Uncle Jimmy. They were married until he passed away. They had a set of twin boys and a daughter. They lived in Baltimore, Maryland, after moving from Raleigh, North Carolina.

(Aunt Billie)

Aunt Lola was a very classy lady and was always properly dressed. She was married to Uncle Lonnie, an engineer for Southern Railways. They were married until his death. They had a set of twin girls and a daughter. They lived in Raleigh, North Carolina.

(Aunt Lola)

Aunt Mae was married to Uncle Moses, a preacher. She became an ordained minister herself. They were married until his death. They had a son who also became a preacher. She was killed in a car accident when she was in her eighties. They lived in the Smithfield area.

(Aunt Mae)

Hazel was the third to the youngest of all the Jordan girls. She was married to Herman (daddy), and had six children: four girls and two boys.

(Hazel - mama in her twenties)

Virginia, or "Johnnie," as everyone calls her, is still living at the age of eighty-nine years and lives in Kenly, North Carolina. She is hilarious and is always cracking everyone up! She has been married three times, and while married to Uncle Bert they had a son named Bert Jr. She had another son named Bobby, by a previous marriage. She always wore high heel shoes and made sure she had lipstick on.

(Aunt "Johnnie")

Aunt Alma was the youngest of the children and was also very pretty; she married Uncle Bill. She was killed in a car accident at an early age of twenty-six. They had a son and a daughter. They lived in Georgia.

(Aunt Alma in her twenties)

"Aunts are good for lifelong memories that'll make you smile just at the thought of them!"

Mama and Uncle Ruffin were very close siblings. He was a jokester and we always liked to kid him.

(Uncle Ruffin with mama)

Uncle Charlie was handsome and the women loved him. We younger children would sneak around and check up on him whenever he had a lady around. We once followed them into the hay barn and were laughing at them playing around in the hay. They noticed us and ran us away, giggling. Uncle Charlie passed away at a young adult age.

(Uncle Charlie)

Uncle Buddy was bald-headed and had a "cocked eye." He could give us looks that were so hilarious, we would laugh out loud! We loved all our "Jordan" aunts and uncles.

(Uncle Buddy peering over the shoulders
of Aunt Johnnie, Aunt Lola, and Aunt Mae)

As of this writing, all of my aunts and uncles in the Canady and Jordan families have passed away with the exception of Aunt Johnnie.

CHAPTER 4

WHO CAN SAY when we actually begin remembering happenings in our childhood? Some people have remembered as far back as two years old, but there are others who remember very little about their entire childhood; blocking it all out.

I was given the gift of remembering as far back as being in my crib; I had an umbilical hernia, which required surgery just before I was two years of age. I remember being in the hospital in my crib, at the hospital, trying to see my mama and daddy through the one-way window. I could only see their shadows and was crying to get to them. My sisters told me I could never remember this, because I was too young. But, I recall the room I was in and the way it looked with other cribs next to mine.

When I was three years old, we younger kids would run all over the neighborhood in the Raleigh area. We lived close to the capitol building and I would go over there to play with the pigeons. Mama found lice on me once when I came home, so she would never allow me to go back to see my pet pigeon. I would cry to go back to see it because I had a love for birds.

When I was around three or four years old, we would go to a nearby banana factory in Raleigh to steal bananas off the conveyor belt. Once, a worker saw us, called out to us, and we all quickly ran down a steep embankment. I fell on a piece of glass and cut my bare foot. It bled all the way back home (I still have the one-inch scar on my foot). That was the last time we ever went back to the banana factory.

(Me, Alice Faye, Sonny Boy, Jo, and Pat)   *(Sonny Boy at one-year old)*

Another one of my earliest childhood memories was while living in Raleigh with our Aunt Billie and her husband, Uncle Jimmy. They had turned their home into apartment units and we rented a room. We didn't have a bath or kitchen, so we had to use their facilities. Once, I turned on the faucet, and while the water was running out of the sink and onto the bathroom floor, I came running down the hall screaming, *"I tut tha rata on and tank tit tha toper off!"* This is when I acquired my nickname: "Tut-Tut." My sisters still call me by my nickname.

I was diagnosed as being "tongue-tied," at the age of three years. Eventually, I needed to have my tongue clipped underneath.

To this day, my sisters still tease me, saying I still have my speech impediment! I just claim that it's only my southern accent.

Ole times there are not forgotten . . .

CHAPTER 5

GARNER, NORTH CAROLINA, is where we lived when my sister, Pat, began school. Whenever she would come home from school with goodies I would cry and insist that mama make her share it with me, and most of the time it worked. I've always been told by my sisters that mama spoiled me as a child.

Pat spent most of her time at my Granny Jordan's house. My Grandpa Jordan always seemed to be partial to Pat. . . maybe that's another reason I never really got close to him?

Pat and I were always doing mischief things together, and we did our share of fussing and fighting, too. So many times, I remember saying to her and her repeating back to me, "I hate you, and wish you were dead!" But, no one else, other than our brothers and sisters, better say that to any of us!

Once, when mama had baked a pan of homemade biscuits (we always had biscuits to eat, even if we didn't have anything else), she left home to go somewhere with a girlfriend and told us not to get into the biscuits while she was gone. Of course, we didn't listen to her request and proceeded to eat a few of them while crumbling up all the remaining biscuits and putting them in the cat bowls for the cats. We always had stray cats around our houses.

When mama returned, she didn't say a word. She went right into baking another batch of biscuits. When Pat and I asked for one of the newly baked biscuits, mama just handed us the cat's bowl that still had crumbled biscuits and said, "Here, you can have these." We ate the biscuits from the cat's bowl, because we were hungry!

There was a deep creek (depending upon whether it had rained or not) that had a rock bridge over it and we would play around the creek many days. My daddy would go to fish in it while he was drunk. He lost his teeth, once, and without thinking he jumped into the creek to get them. He did not know how to swim, but somehow he managed to crawl out, along with his teeth!

Mama told me that she took me to the movies and I had food on my face and she spit in her hand to clean my face and I spit back at her. She thought it was funny. She also told us that if you wiped your face with a pee diaper, it would help heal the blemishes on your face. (This was most likely another "old wives tale" from granny.) She did wipe her face with a pee diaper a few times.

(Mama, when we lived in Garner, North Carolina.)

Our baby brother, Robert Lee, was my and Pat's little doll. We would dress him up in doll clothes, and I distinctly remember the little red ruffled dress we dressed him in. He was so cute with his bright red hair, looking like a little girl. We enjoyed playing as if we were his mama, feeding him and rocking him to sleep.

One day, while he was asleep in his crib, I went into his room and there were flies on him and flying all around him. I ran and got the DDT spray can that we used to kill insects and sprayed it all over his head and on his crib. I felt good that I had killed all the flies.

His head quickly became red and infected with blisters all over it from the DDT spray. He was taken to the doctor after mama and daddy couldn't figure out what was causing it. When he returned home, his head was covered with a dark purple medicine and he looked like a little monster. I fessed up to mama and daddy what I had done, and told them that I was only trying to keep the flies off of him! They couldn't be angry with me for that!

To this day, Robert Lee blames me for his premature baldness, but I say that he just inherited his baldness from Uncle Buddy.

CHAPTER 6

WE LIVED IN many houses; most of them where "black" (unpainted), high off the ground, with no foundation. We always referred to all the houses we'd lived in by the names of the landlords. We moved around so often that it's hard to figure out exact dates and ages. So, I have only my faded memories to try to tie our experiences together.

One particular home was a log house with no electricity in the White Lake area of North Carolina. It was around Easter time, because I remember hiding Easter eggs in that yard. (I can't recall the name of this home's landlord.) This home had dirt floors, with a linoleum rug over the dirt. We were constantly sweeping the dirt off the linoleum back onto the outside edges. The log house had four rooms, one being the pack room. It had a stone fireplace in the front room.

There was an old organ in the pack room and Pat and I had fun playing on the organ and performing, with our own kind of music, dancing, and singing. We would pretend to be on stage and entertaining an audience (our little brothers).

We would go to White Lake to swim and play. Once, while mama was drinking alcohol, she fell into the water at White Lake with her clothes on. A preacher was there at the time, and mama's dress floated up over her head when she fell in. She couldn't swim so the preacher helped her out of the water. Not only had the preacher seen her after she had been drinking, but had seen her with her dress over her head!

We didn't live in this house very long before we moved to another house.

CHAPTER 7

THIS NEXT HOUSE was called the "JD Cobb" house. It was cinder-block and located at the edge of a swamp. We would wade through the dark waters every chance we got, using the murky water to make our mud pies. We enjoyed jumping and rolling in mud holes, too.

We would climb up in the "chaney ball" tree in our backyard and go potty to see who could make the biggest splat on the ground. This was the same tree that was used by daddy, Uncle Ruffin, and their friends to hang hogs to cut and clean.

We would watch as they would hang the hogs and cut them open to drain all the guts and blood out. Then they would cut them up into pieces and distribute the meat among themselves, for cooking. We would watch mama as she would run some of the meat through a grinder to make sausage. We got a lot of sausage, but never got much bacon.

We kids always had to make our own kind of entertainment. We played a lot of games: hide-and-seek; "One, two, three; coming, ready or not"; "There ain't no bugger bears out tonight, grandpa killed them all last night"; hopscotch; and jumping rope using grape vines.

One of our favorite things to do was to play "doodle bug." There would be tiny holes in the ground and we would take a small twig and twirl it around in the ground saying, "Doodle bug, doodle bug, come out tonight. Your house is on fire!" We would quickly pull it out and there would be a small grub worm on the end of the stick. We got many laughs from this.

We would get a kick out of turning over the old run-down

outhouse. We would turn it over, laughing, and then go run and hide, leaving everyone to wonder who had done it. Our old outhouse sat high off the ground. Sometimes, we would just go to the back of it and squat, if needed. I was always afraid to sit down on it because of spiders, so I would always just squat on it. From the kitchen doorway, you could see who would squat behind it! Once, we were laughing at our Aunt Eula Mae (Uncle Ruffin's wife) while she was peeing behind the outhouse, swatting at the flies!

Daddy would go gigging for frogs in the swamp and bring them home to fry frog legs. We would laugh when they would almost jump out of the frying pan. We loved eating frog legs. They tasted a lot like fried chicken. We would use daddy's gig tool to chase each other around the yard, pretending we were the devil.

I don't remember ever seeing snakes while we played in the swamplands. However, daddy came home one night stating that he had accidently picked up a water moccasin while he was gigging. Mama was concerned with him going out in the swampy waters while he was drinking alcohol, but he seemed to always return unharmed.

Granny Jordan lived nearby the JD Cobb house and we would walk to her house through the woods. She always had good food on the table (also covered with a tablecloth) for us to eat. She would have biscuits and jellies sitting out for us. I loved going to see Granny Jordan.

Once, we were over at Granny Jordan's house and Uncle Buddy was drunk and trying to climb a tree with the tractor; he almost flipped it! Granny was out there boiling clothes in a black kettle over hot coals and called out, "Get off that tractor, you fool!" We were told never to call anyone a "fool"; it was granny so it was okay.

My sister, Pat, would squeeze the boils on Grandpa Jordan's back and it would gross me out! Since she lived with Granny and Grandpa Jordan more than she stayed at home at times, I feel this is the reason I spent more time with my brothers while growing up. It seemed I was too young for my older sisters, Jo and Alice Faye. There's only two and three years between my brothers' ages and mine, so we were playmates and buddies. I suppose you could have called me a little tomboy, too.

When our little brother, Sonny Boy, was still in diapers, he would call Alice Faye, "mama." He would follow her around the house and he considered her his mama. We thought it was really cute to see him following her around and crying after her.

We liked going to the cotton fields and enjoyed being able to ride on the back of the tractor and trailer at the end of the day's work. On one particular evening, after work, we all climbed on the back of a long-bed trailer for a ride home. The tractor was being driven by mama; the trailer was loaded with bags of cotton. We were all laughing, singing, and having fun, when all of a sudden we felt a big bump! Everyone said, "What was that?" We thought maybe we had just run over a rock or something.

After a few seconds of wondering and looking around, we saw that Sonny Boy was missing from the trailer. We started yelling for mama to stop the tractor, but she couldn't hear us. Finally, daddy jumped down from the trailer and ran up to her to stop it. We looked back and saw our brother's little body lying on the road! We all began to cry and were screaming and running back to him, hoping and praying that he wasn't dead!

He was turning grey and gasping for breath! Immediately, our neighbor picked him up and put him in his car and rushed him to the local hospital. We waited and waited—it seemed for hours wondering if he would die.

Finally, we got the word that he was going to be okay; the wheels of the trailer had run over his stomach, so it hadn't broken any bones and he had no internal injuries! We were so happy to hear that he would be okay. He was hospitalized for a few days and when he return from the hospital, Sonny Boy was still calling Alice Faye, "mama." I can still see him running around in his diaper after her. He would rather be going nude most of the time, however.

Pat, Sonny Boy, and I would climb up on the top of Robert Lee's crib to climb into the attic. Once we were up there, we were playing hide-and-seek when I stepped on a rusty nail with my bare foot. After seeing the blood, I began to scream like I was dying! I never went to the doctor for it; mama just put alcohol on it, and eventually, it healed. We never worried about blood poison, in those days.

We would get inside the large tractor wheels that weren't being used (sometimes two of us at a time) and start at the top of the steepest hill and roll down the hill until something would stop us! Sometimes, it was a ditch, but most of the time it would be a bush or a tree.

CHAPTER 8

OUR NEXT HOUSE was the "McMillan" house. Mama had never cut my hair and it had grown long. It would always be tangled up and I would cry when she would comb it. I was so tender headed that I would cry each time. Mama would get so frustrated with me when she combed it. My two older sisters, Jo and Alice Faye, say they were always jealous of me because mama seemed to always be combing my hair.

All of us girls had long, straight hair. Mama would dampen our hair and then cut up brown paper bags into small strips to curl it. This would be done by folding the strips and twirling our hair into them prior to our going to bed at night. The next morning we would have a head full of curls (the Shirley Temple look). Jo and Alice Faye got tired of my hair being combed and one day, when I was five years old, they cut my hair off above my ears. They told me how pretty it looked. I thought it was beautiful at first, but mama saw what they had done and she became so angry that she spanked them. I realized it must not have been so beautiful. She insisted that they take me to school with them the next day, to embarrass them. When I boarded the bus, they didn't seem to be embarrassed as much as I was. This happened prior to my starting school, so, I didn't really have any classmates at school to tease me.

I began school while we were living at the McMillan house, though. One of my most embarrassing days at school was when I was in the first grade. I went to school without any underwear on. While I was boarding the bus, one of the kids saw up my dress and started laughing at me and making fun of me. I was so embarrassed and upset that I came home, crying. I can still recall the little yellow and white dress I had on that day. From then on, mama always made sure I had underwear on (even if I had to borrow a pair of my sisters'), although we never had a lot of underwear. We always wore each other's clothes, sometimes too big and sometimes too small. Whatever we could find to wear, we would wear. I think I even wore some of my brother's clothes. I always had to wear hand-me-downs from my brothers and sisters.

One day at school, I had a new little friend, Nancy, and she had the largest and prettiest red apple I had ever seen. When she wasn't looking, I took my scarf and covered the apple and put it in my desk. When she told the teacher that someone had stolen her apple, the teacher began checking all the children's desks. I was so nervous watching her go from desk to desk checking for the apple. When she got to mine, I picked up my scarf covering the apple and held it in my hand. She never said a word to me, but I do believe she saw that I had the apple. My little hand just couldn't shield an apple that big. I kept it in my desk until school was out, then took it home and shared it with my little brothers.

We were not fortunate enough to eat fresh fruit—except maybe the ones off apple trees that may be around our house, and they usually had worms in them. It was unusual to have fruit around the house (even around Christmas time).

When you are young and poor, you don't miss having material things because you don't know any better. We kids were happy in our lives at that time, it seemed. Since we had no new toys to play with we would make do with swinging in tires tied on tree limbs and swinging as high as possible. We would also climb trees and swing over creeks on the grape vines in the woods. A branch off of a tree or a tobacco stick was our kind of toy. We would build houses with tobacco sticks and climb up the side and over the top to get inside it. We would make a walking stick out of tobacco sticks and we loved to climb up on it and walk around the yard that mama had just raked, and she would get upset with us for messing up her yard.

I never had a bike, and to this day I do not know how to ride a bike, especially the fancy ones. I do remember having a scooter that we all had to share. I never figured out where we got it, though.

I would run with a curtain rod, pushing it in front of me. Once, I hit a rock and the rod stabbed me in the shin. It went deep into my skin, almost to the bone. We just washed it and stopped the bleeding. Mama would use Vicks Vapor Rub on almost any sores, and for colds. She would put a glob of Mentholatum on her finger and stick it down our throat and rub Vick's Vapor Rub on our chests when we had sore throats. To this day, I use Vick's Vapor Rub as a cure for many of my ailments.

I never remembered going to the doctor's office as a child. We would get cuts and scratches and mama would stop the bleeding and cover it with Mercurochrome that had a mixture of 30 percent alcohol. It burned and we would cry, but it seemed to work and it never got infected.

At the age of six years old, Pat and I had our tonsils taken out at the same time. When we went into the hospital for surgery, she was taken into surgery first. When she came out of surgery she was screaming and kicking and fighting the nurses. It scared me so bad that when they came for me I jumped out of bed and ran and jumped under another bed. They had to literally drag me out from under the bed and tie me down to take me into the operating room.

I was scratching, screaming, and kicking when they slapped a pad filled with ether over my nose. I felt like I was smothering! After taking one breath of the ether, I felt like I was in a large tunnel and there were circles going round and round in my head! I still can't tolerate the smell of ether.

We always heard that if you go into surgery calm, you will come out fighting and if you go in fighting, you will come out calm. That's exactly how it happened with us. I can still relate to the awful soreness from the surgery. The only good thing about having your tonsils out is that you get a lot of popsicles and Jell-O to eat.

The McMillan house was located on a large farm with a long dirt path leading up to its doors. This house is one of the most vivid places we ever lived. It was located in the middle of a farm owned by the McMillan family. The long path to our house connected one paved highway to another main highway.

The McMillan family was very well known around the area. We thought they were rich! They lived in a big white house with all the amenities. They were hard-working farmers and nice folks. They owned a lot of acreage and raised peanuts, cotton, potatoes, corn, watermelon, tomatoes, and other vegetables. Most likely the farm had tobacco on it, too, since we always had tobacco sticks around, and North Carolina is "tobacco country."

Our homes never had many trees in the yards, since they were located in the middle of farmland. There was only one tree in our yard that we would climb and then we would go into the woods to find other trees. We would play "Tarzan," swinging from the scuppernong grape vines (these are large grapes that grow wild in the South). Mama would even climb the trees at times to get the large grapes for us to eat.

I remember the smell of the morning glories, honeysuckles, and the maroon red flowers on the, "sweet bubby" bushes. The scientific name for the Sweet Bubby bush is Calycanthus floridus, but we always called them "sweet bubby" bushes. Their blossoms had the sweetest aroma. I still look for them when I go back to visit North Carolina. (I've even planted a couple in my yard, nowadays.)

(Sweet bubby bloom)

I love the "molly-pops" flower, which has a beautiful ballerina dancing in the middle of the flower. This flower symbolizes elements of the passion of the Lord: the lacy crown could be a halo or crown of thorns; the five stamens the five wounds; the ten petal-like parts the ten faithful apostles. The scientific name for this plant is Passiflora.

(Molly pop flower)

I've always enjoyed the smell of the forest in the South, especially after a rain. There's nothing more refreshing than that smell at dusk and the clean smell in the early morning hours.

Whenever I go visit and travel through the South, I lower my car windows just to inhale the aroma of the forest, taking me back to my early childhood days.

There were dogwood trees in the woods around our house. Mama would tell us that the dogwood tree was a "religious" tree, too. The flower represented the cross that Jesus was nailed to. The middle of the flower was the thorns he wore around his head, and then the tips of the pedals were the blood stains from his blood. The four pedals represent the cross. I have continued to relate that story to my children and others.

(Dog wood flower)

There was a nice family who lived on the same path to our house. We would go visit them because they had children the same ages as my older sisters. The owner passed away with a heart attack while he, daddy, and others were out hunting. We all went to their home to view him in his casket. Back in those days, in the South, families would have the deceased lay in their home for viewing instead of at a funeral home. That was the first time I had ever seen a dead person. I had a few nightmares after that. To this day, I can still picture him in the casket and hearing the coo-coo clock above the fireplace, cooing-cooing as we stood over him.

The cemetery where he was buried was very close to our house. We kids would walk over to the cemetery and take pretty flowers and ribbons off some of the graves to put in our playhouses. We were always looking for a way to spiff up our playhouses. Those beautiful yellow, pink, and red ribbons really made our playhouses beautiful!

It was not uncommon to see graveyards in people's backyards, in those days.

Being poor, we were always hungry, and food was forever on our minds. We would steal watermelons and peanuts from the McMillan farm and eat them right out of the field. At times we would get deathly sick from eating warm watermelons (or maybe too much of them). I think of the many times I leaned over the porch, barfing, and having a bad case of diarrhea due to eating too much of the stolen food. Surprisingly, to this day watermelon is one of my favorite foods. Peanuts were also one of our favorite foods to steal, and sometimes we would eat them for our only meal. We would pull up raw peanuts and eat them right out of the ground, dirt and all.

It is hard to imagine that daddy, having so little education, could have fed a wife and six kids. By our living on farms, we were blessed to at least have vegetables (cooked or raw).

There were vegetables in the fields and chickens in the yard and we would sometimes get them, but many times we had to fend for ourselves for something to eat. Mama and daddy would be too busy with their ups and downs, or they would be away from the home.

Once in a blue moon, when we would have supper together, it was always a rush to see who would get the last biscuit. It still rings in my ears, my brother, Sonny Boy, saying, "Pass the biscuits, please." At times we would put together biscuits and syrup or just plain biscuits and sugar for our meals and lunches for my older sisters to take to school.

I have always said that mama could put a meal together with nothing and as long as she had flour. She would cook chicken over and over, getting the broth for another dish, etc. She would make many meals with chicken and dumplings. Mama never really learned to cook that well, though.

Mama never worked outside of the home in a public job. She had only worked in the fields. I feel she tried to be a good mama to us kids, whenever we had her full attention and she and daddy weren't arguing and fighting; this was very seldom, though.

Our homes were always sparsely decorated. This house was a four-bedroom house: kitchen/dining area, two bedrooms, and an extra pack room. The kitchen/dining area had a wood stove, picnic table and china chest. One bedroom had a bed, dresser, and an oil stove (I would climb up on it to try to keep warm). This room was daddy and mama's bedroom. The other bedroom had two beds in it, a double bed and a single bed; this room was for all of us kids. We would get cold at night and would sleep three of us at the head of the double bed and three of us at the foot of it.

One of my sisters was a "bed wetter" and we always tried to protect her from getting in trouble. We would move our little brother, Robert Lee, to her spot and say it was him. He wouldn't get in trouble, being he was the baby. Although, once, I had an accident and traded places with her to keep me from getting whipped. . . still feeling a little guilty about that one!

The pack room was the only place to put our clothing, because we didn't have closets or drawers. All our clothes were in piles on the floor. This was also the room that the "pee pot" was placed in, since we had no bathroom with running water.

When mama would have enough of daddy's abuse, she would leave. Daddy would sometimes bring home weird people. Once, he brought a man home who was dressed up like a woman. His name was Melvin and he was strange looking, wearing women's clothing and lipstick. I never figured out what that was all about? When I think back on it now, Melvin must have been a gay man. In those days you never heard about gays. My daddy was such a womanizer; it is hard to think that he could have been bi-sexual. The two of them would just sit around drinking, laughing and talking until they would sooner or later pass out.

Daddy was associated with one of the very famous bootleggers, Percy Flowers (and his brother, Johnny). He would drive us all over to Percy's home to pick up "white lightning" (moonshine liquor) to drink. Percy and his brother, later, spent many years in the penitentiary for bootlegging, which was illegal in Johnston County.

Daddy was spending all his hard-earned money (the little he had) on buying booze. . . but sometimes he was given "free" whiskey. This made it even more convenient for him to drink and stay away from home.

Me, Pat, and my two brothers went into Mr. McMillan's family home, while they were away once and opened the refrigerator and drank their milk, ate some grapes, and I ran my fingers through a lemon meringue pie. Lemon meringue pie was then and still is my favorite pie! I also stole a couple of small artificial "peeps" (the kind you get at Easter time).

We pulled many flowers from their "snowball" bushes to decorate our playhouse. We had never seen such beautiful white flowers! Our mama liked zinnias and that was the type of flower we were more accustomed to having in our yard. There was also another flower that mama had in our yard that she would boil in hot water to make tea from it. It was a red flower, and to this day we can't determine the type of flower it was.

The McMillan's were such nice people; I'm sure they would have shared the milk, pie, and the flowers with us if we had asked for them. They did say we could come and get grapes anytime we wanted.

After the McMillan family arrived back home, Mr. McMillan walked up the path to our house to talk to our daddy. Of course, when we saw him coming we all ran to hide, knowing we were in big trouble!

Daddy called us in and insisted that we return everything that we had taken back to them and apologize. We could take everything back, but apologizing to them was out of the question! We laid the flowers, little peeps, and other small items on the front porch and ran back up the path to our house, without saying a word to them.

After we returned home, he cussed at us and gave us a leather-belt whipping. We were always doing things that upset our daddy. This one whipping taught me, however, to never take anything that didn't belong to me!

We would crawl under the house and sweep the ground down to hardpan soil, clearing an area to make a play house. It seemed to be a safe haven for us little ones. Making a playhouse seemed to be the best thing to do to occupy our time. We loved to play mama and daddy and pretend to be a normal family (or what we thought to be a normal family).

Once, when I was swinging on the doors of the china cabinet in our kitchen, the whole cabinet turned over and fell on me! All the dishes, glasses, etc. fell out all over the floor. I thought I was hurt bad, but I was too frightened to feel anything and too eager to get up and run to think about the dishes being broken.

Daddy came in, cussing and raving, "What the hell is going on!" It scared the "daylights" out of me and I ran outside and hid under the house. Knowing what was going to happen to me I figured I better come out and take what was coming, or it would be worse. When daddy began hitting me with the belt I screamed like I was dying. (We would always scream loud to make daddy stop hitting us.) It seemed to work, sometimes. But, it really hurt worse when we got hit by the buckle. We were afraid of daddy, especially when he was drinking, holding a belt and more so with a gun.

I don't remember mama ever whipping me. If she had, I'm sure it would have been with a switch. Granny Jordan sure would take a switch to us but then, I'm sure we probably deserved it.

It's hard for me to understand how my mama was able to handle all six of us kids. She always seemed to make sure we were clean, though. She would pump water into the tub or let it fill up with rain water (the same tub she would use to wash our clothes in). She would let it sit in the sun to warm the water.

We would argue over who would be the first one to bathe. Of course, the older ones would get first choice. When we didn't take baths in the tub, we would have to take sponge baths. (Sponge baths are with little water, a washcloth, and soap.)

There was an elderly lady who lived off another dirt road from our house, and she would come visit us. We would sit on the porch with her and she would tell us stories. She wore long rubber underwear and always chewed on a sassafras root and dipped snuff with it. She seemed to be a little weird, but she showed Pat and me where to look and how to find the sassafras roots in the woods.

A sassafras root smells like root beer and comes from the root of a sassafras bush or tree. We would chew on them and pretend we were dipping snuff, too. We did this for such a long period of time that I became nauseous from the smell and taste of root beer. Now, as an adult, however, root beer floats are one of my favorite desserts.

We were keeping a bunch of baby chicks in the shed, and when we awoke one morning to go out to feed them we found that the wharf rats had killed them and some had even been eaten. We had huge rats around our house! On another occasion, a snake had gotten into the chicken coop and had eaten some of the chicken eggs.

We would go barefoot most of the time, and so many times we had to clean chicken poop out from between our toes. I'm surprised I don't have webbed feet now, because of how often I went barefoot.

One day, daddy brought home an icebox (a refrigerator without electricity). Wow, we were excited to be able to have ice, although the ice was to keep the refrigerator cold! Robert Lee, Sonny Boy, Pat, and I would use it as a hiding place when we would play hide-and-seek. Sometimes, we would hold the door shut just to hear the other ones scream to get out. We never understood the danger in doing this.

I had always been told that, "God takes care of children and drunks." I suppose God had his hands full with our family! I am so thankful God was watching over us because it didn't seem as if any-one else was.

Later, daddy brought home a washing machine and we thought it was great that mama would not have to wash clothes on a wash-board and tub any more. Of course, we thought this wringer/washer machine could possibly be a toy, too!

While playing with the washer, one day, Pat got her hand caught in the wringer (the part that squeezes the water out of the cloths). The wringer rolled up to Pat's wrist before mama came in to help her get hand out of it. Things like this were always happening around our house. We just tried to make fun and games out of everything we could find.

We must have looked like a bunch of wild kids to the neighbors! We were always running around the neighborhood. We ran through the woods and we walked for miles to the store for one-cent candy or a piece of gum.

One day, while walking along the highway, I looked down and picked up what I thought was a balloon. We began taking turns, blowing it up and watching it get bigger and bigger. It was the largest balloon we had ever seen! We would fill it with water to see just how big it would get. We played with it for a long time, until mama came out of the house and saw it! She almost fainted when she realized it was a used condom. We didn't understand, at the time, why she had gotten so upset. She made us throw it away immediately. To think of it, now . . . yikes!

Mama was hanging out clothes one evening, as the sun was setting, and she nearly stepped on a copperhead snake! She got a hoe and chopped its head off. It is hard to believe that, of all the times we played in the woods and under the house, the snakes didn't bother us. They must have been just as afraid of us as we were of them!

To this day, I am terrified of snakes! I still tell everyone about all the venomous snakes in North Carolina. Every snake that I had ever seen or been told about throughout my childhood had been venomous: copperheads, cottonmouths, rattlesnakes. Maybe the snake that ate all our chicken eggs wasn't venomous, though? All I know is that any snake to us was venomous, and, "a good snake is a dead snake!"

We had always heard about the "black racer" snake. I try to tell people about it now and they just laugh at me. It was believed that a "black racer" would roll up in a ball or a ring and chase you. That was, most likely, another one of the tales my Granny Jordan told us. She was a wonderful story teller. With all her scary and ghostly tales she told, I am surprise that we aren't mentally warped from them.

My Grandpa Jordan was part Cherokee Indian and couldn't hold his booze well. Sometimes, when he would be drinking and acting up, Granny Jordan would say, "Don't mind John, he was just released from Dix Hill." (Dix Hill was an insane asylum in Raleigh, North Carolina.) We would just laugh at her, knowing she was kidding.

Soon after daddy had gotten the icebox and washing machine, he brought home a car! It was a "Woody," station wagon. We would play in the car, pretending to be driving and messing around with the controls. Once, the cigarette lighter began smoking and almost caught fire. We called mama and she had to scrape the stuff out of it that we had stuffed in it. We were scolded, but not whipped.

Daddy tried to teach mama to drive the Woody. Once, while she was driving up the long dirt path to our house, another car turned onto the driveway headed toward her and she panicked and turned off the path, going across the open field. He never tried teaching her again and she never insisted that he do it, either. She never learned to drive a car.

We loved to hear Granny Jordan tell ghost stories and talk about the "spirits" and dead people. We would say, "Scare us, granny, scare us again!" The more we begged her to scare us, the scarier her stories got. Since Granny Jordan was married to an Indian, she had heard a lot of Indian tales and passed them on to us. When there was a full moon, granny would say it was a "spirit," and that ghosts come to see us as a big bright ball in the air. The full moon always seemed to shine behind our outhouse. Needless to say, we would never go near the outhouse at night. That's another reason we always kept the "pee pot" in the pack room.

Granny Jordan would tell us superstitions: never walk under a ladder; never walk on a crack in the sidewalk; never split a pole when walking with someone else; beware if a black cat crosses your path; when there is a ring around the moon, It means rain Is on the way; when birds sit on power lines, they are waiting for snow; when snow lays on the ground for days, another snow is coming; and when it rains while the sun is shining, the devil's beating his wife. We believed every one of those superstitions because Granny Jordan said so!

Our mama had a carefree personality; she was passive, friendly, petite, and a pretty woman. I remember her laughing, singing, and crying. She enjoyed singing and dancing around the house with a broom or mop when daddy wasn't home and we would run and dance around with her.

(Mama in her twenties)

Mama and her brother, Uncle Ruffin, would sing "Paper Roses," and Ernest Tubb's, "I'm Walking the Floor over You," recorded in 1948. Ernest Tubb was born on February 2, 1914 and died on September 6, 1984. I never realized that he was the first singer to record the hit version of "Blue Christmas." I always thought Elvis had made that song famous. Ernest Tubb was mama's favorite country singer.

Mama would play little "singsong" games with us, like, *"Two little birdies sitting on the fence, one named Jack and one named Jill. Fly away, Jack, fly away, Jill. Come back, Jack, come back, Jill."* She would put a piece of paper on a finger of each hand and then behind her back would change to a finger that didn't have the paper and then say, "Fly away, Jack, fly away, Jill", and change it back to the finger with the paper and then say, "Come back, Jack, come back, Jill." It took us a long time to figure out how she did this. I took this game with me throughout my life and have shared it with my children and grandchildren.

Daddy was a spit fire, especially when he was drunk; he had the devil in him. Even when he was sober, he was "ill as a hornet", as we would say. He was a small-framed, handsome man, but had an uncontrollable temper. He cussed a lot and drank a lot of whisky (or anything he could find), and to this day I can't tolerate the smell of whisky, or to hear the "G-D D-m" expression (that was his favorite expression when he was angry).

(Daddy)

With my daddy's personality and his ill temper, he never had any patience with us kids. He was always saying, "You can't ever have a damn thing when you have kids!" I do understand, now, why he thought that way, because we broke things around our home that most people couldn't break, even if they tried to! However, we never broke a bone, which is remarkable since we climbed every tree we could find, and climbed and jumped off every rooftop of our houses and barns. We did have many scrapes and bruises, however.

It's not who my daddy was, but who I think he was that matters. I don't believe my daddy even liked kids. I can't remember ever sitting on my daddy's lap or having him read to me or tucking me in at bedtime. I don't believe he knew how to be loving and caring to us. Maybe he felt trapped? He would have really felt trapped had he ended up with eight kids (counting mama's two miscarriages) instead of six!

We were exposed to and had seen things during our childhood that no child should have ever had to see.

There was a cotton field next to our house. I loved to pick cotton with mama and help her carry her cotton sack that hung over her shoulder by a strap. Sometimes, I would just drag it behind her. I really liked to pick the fluffy balls of cotton. You could, however, get your fingers pricked if the cotton ball wasn't ready to be picked. I also liked to ride on the back of the cotton sled that pulled behind a tractor, when they would come around to pick up the full bags.

One day, I was in the cotton field with mama and Robert Lee and Sonny Boy were playing outside, my sisters were in school and daddy came driving up the dirt path yelling for mama to go home. By the tone of his voice, I became nervous and upset because he seemed mad about something. I would always get nervous when daddy would raise his voice around our house.

Later, when I ran up to the house, he was fighting with mama and telling her she had been cheating on him, asking her where she had been all day. He was yelling at her and calling her a whore, a bitch, and all sorts of bad names. This was one of the worst times I had ever seen my daddy and mama fighting.

I was crying and telling daddy that mama and I had been in the fields all day, picking cotton. He began beating on her and all she would do was raise her arms over her head to protect herself and cry.

I ran crying and hid in our playhouse, under the house. I always felt that daddy would do wrong things outside of our home and then come home and take his guilt out on mama. I was always afraid that he would sooner or later kill her!

My sister, Alice Faye, seemed to be the only one of us who could make daddy settle down when he would go into a drunken rage. She was strong as an ox and didn't take any of his BS when he was drinking. However, she wasn't around on this particular day.

When he would start fighting with mama and going into a rage, Jo would say, "Alice, please make them stop, please make them stop!" The rest of us were too young to ever do anything.

Daddy and mama were married when they were in their teens and we have always been told that they were so in love; these two people should have never gotten together. They were very jealous of each other and it showed every minute of every day.

Daddy was an alcoholic and mama became one, too, but she always said she never began drinking until after she met him. She would drink as heavy as he did, at times.

We were always running outside to get away from them when they would begin to argue, knowing that fighting would soon follow. When they fought, it would end up with one of them leaving home (most of the time it would be daddy); sometimes, staying away for days.

Daddy beat mama so many times, and once, he beat her until she was unconscious. All I could think of, even at that young age, was that he must really hate my mama to be so mean to her. Mama usually had bruises on her body that showing the abuse. In today's time, he would have been locked up in jail, but this was in the 1940s and things were different then. Mama was unable to call the police because we never had a telephone; she could only leave home to get away from him. It seemed that each time one of them left, he would end up apologizing saying he will never do it again. They would make up until the next time.

I wish mama had been stronger and that she would have had the means to be able to stand up to him, but my mama was afraid of him and she didn't like conflict. Most of their arguments seemed to be instigated by daddy. Whatever the reasons for their arguing, I knew then that I would never want to be around someone who treated me the way he treated my mama.

Once, when mama left home, she took me with her. We boarded a bus to Atlanta, Georgia, to see her sister and her husband: Aunt Alma and Uncle Bill. Being that I did not have a middle name, Aunt Alma always wanted mama to make my middle name, "Alma." We began just saying my middle name would be "Alma." However, my birth certificate was never changed to reflect the change.

Mama and I were away from home for quite a while. Once, while at Aunt Alma's house, Bill, Jr. and I were playing and he got mad at me. He began hitting me and Uncle Bill told him to stop it and Bill Jr.

said, "Can I pull her hair, though?" They thought it was funny. I never realized that it would be the last time I would see my Aunt Alma. She was killed in a car accident in the late 1940s. She was only twenty-six years old at the time of her death.

(The Canady Girls, AKA the Jordan Girls)

Jo

Alice Faye

Pat

Jerrie

CHAPTER 9

THE "ATKINSON" HOME was located near a large pond. We would walk down a long, dirt road to the old bridge over the river that ran into Cattail Pond. The bridge had old boards with big cracks showing the flowing waters underneath. I was afraid to walk across the bridge so I would get down on my hands and knees and crawl across. My siblings would laugh at me crawling across it.

The Atkinson house sat high off the ground. There was an open well in the front yard where we would draw water. This home was located on a rocky dirt road. It had four rooms, and, of course, it had a pack room. Daddy and mama's bed was located in the living room and the kids' beds were all in one room. Again, there was no indoor bathroom or running water.

To the right of the front porch was an old rundown black shack with two rooms. We always thought it must have been used for slaves' quarters, once. We used it as a playhouse (it allowed us to play out of the rain and snow). We would, sometimes, use the potty through the floor planks that were missing, for our bathroom. Not having a bathroom in the house, we would use whatever we could find when nature called.

To the left of the front porch there was an old, two-story barn with an old horse in the stable. It must have been the landlord's horse. We would play hide-and-seek in the hay loft. Daddy would use the horse to plow the fields around our house. I remember seeing him plow the fields with the horse's strap around his shoulders and sweating all the way.

On a path leading up from the barn was a gravesite with one lonely tree for shade. We would go to the gravesite and sit and tell some of Granny Jordan's ghostly tales. When we didn't have Granny Jordan around to tell us stories, we would make up our own scary ones. Our sister, Alice Faye, told us that if you poked a fork in the grave, the dead would pull you into the ground with the casket. We would stab it with a fork and then take off running and screaming.

Mama would lay old bed springs out in the yard and cover it with gunny sacks, so we could jump on it and pretend it was a trampoline—that is, when we weren't running through the woods, jumping rope with grape vines, playing hopscotch, or swinging from a tree in a rubber tire. We must have climbed every tree in the woods around the houses we lived. (We also made playhouses up in trees.) We would climb anything, and must have looked like a family of monkeys to all our neighbors.

Once, when daddy was drunk, he went outside and killed a possum and brought it home to BBQ. That was food on the table! We would eat possum, bird, squirrel, rabbit, and most anything he could shoot. With all the snakes around, I'm surprised we never ate snake!

One night, he brought a possum home in a gunny sack and left it lying on the kitchen table. The next morning, the possum was missing from the sack. After checking all the areas around the house, daddy found the possum in the bed all snuggled up against Sonny Boy's warm tummy. Mama and daddy were afraid to disturb it, thinking it might bite him. But they finally got up the nerve to grab it by its tail and take it away from its warm sleeping place.

Daddy always worked hard on the farms and, sometimes, I enjoyed going out with him and watching him plow the fields. Remembering back, I believe my daddy was a farmhand and farmed the land for our landlords for free rent.

It seemed the fighting between mama and daddy could always get worse. Daddy would have drinking buddies over and that would eventually create a fight, most likely due to jealousy.

One day, daddy's second cousin, Elmo, and another man were standing around, talking in the front yard. They were intoxicated and Elmo and mama were getting in the truck to leave, while Pat was telling them not to go. She was trying to get into the truck with them and Elmo quickly picked her up and held her upside down over the open well. He threatened to throw her into the well if she didn't leave them alone.

We began yelling at the top of our lungs, "Stop it! Stop it! Don't do it! Let her go!" We were all crying, hysterically. He was laughing and joking about it and the other man insisted that he put her down. We were all terrified and Pat was screaming at the top of her lungs! I have been traumatized many times throughout my youth, but this is one incident that really stands out in my mind!

Sonny Boy was still enjoying taking his clothes off and going nude. Daddy, in a drunken stupor, saw him with his clothes off during a snow storm and picked him up and threw him out in about three feet of snow, thinking this would stop him from running around nude. The rest of us ran out and quickly got him back into the house. It did seem to stop Sonny Boy from going nude, however.

Mama had washed her hair and was curling it, one day, and daddy came inside, saying he was hungry and wanted to eat. She said, "Wait until I finish curling my hair." He said, "Right now!" She continued curling her hair and it angered him. He started cussing at her and yelling for her to get off her ass and make him something to eat. He grabbed her arm and dragged her into the pack room and began beating on her. All we could hear was her crying and things being thrown around and her screaming in pain.

Jo was pleading to Alice Faye to go stop them, and we were all crying and running around, wondering what was going on. Like I've said before, we always thought that someday he was going to kill her . . . now, this could be the time! All of a sudden, there was silence! Our ears were pinned to the door. We could hear him murmuring. Then, daddy walked out and Jo and Alice Faye went in to see if mama was alive.

We found out that daddy had beaten her and had rubbed red pepper on her vagina. He had accused her of being unfaithful to him, once again. This incident was never to be told, although it was one of the most memorable.

CHAPTER 10

WE FELT THAT the "Murchison Road" house was the best house we had ever lived in. It was located in a rural area off Murchison Road in Fayetteville, North Carolina. It was a seven-room home. They were small rooms, but still, they were separate rooms.

It also had a pack room where we kept our clothing, toys, and anything else we wanted to store. Aunt Lola had just given us several boxes of hand-me-down clothes from her three daughters. My sisters always liked to get clothes from Aunt Lola because she always brought such pretty things. Of course, all these boxes went into the pack room.

The house had a screened-in porch, along with two other porches: a front and a back porch. This house was located on one of the busiest highways heading into Fayetteville from Fort Bragg. It did not have a bathroom, only an outhouse. However, it did have a water pump on the back porch (not in the yard).

The electricity had been turned off several times due to nonpayment. However, each time it would be turned off, daddy would go out and "straight wire" it so we would have lights. We had to keep all the windows covered with blankets so the utility company couldn't drive by and see that the electricity was on.

Across the highway were railroad tracks. My brothers, Pat, and I would go over to the railroad tracks to play until we heard the train's whistle. We would wait until the last minute for it to get close to us and then we would take off running. I can still remember the smell of the creosote on the railroad ties. The engineers would throw hard candy out to us as it passed by.

We had always heard that if you put a penny on the railroad tracks and a train ran over it, it would flatten the penny. Of course, we tried it and it worked. The woods were filled with tall North Carolina pine trees. Nothing is more soothing than listening to the wind blowing through the tall Carolina pines.

There was a drainage tunnel that went underneath the highway to the other side and we would crawl through it to get to the tracks. What a surprise when one day while we were crawling through it and found a box full of Almond Joy candy bars! It must have fallen off a truck. Of course we began eating them and after telling mama about finding the box and offering her one to eat, she found that it had worms in it! She took the rest away from us but we found them and ate them all, anyway. It's no wonder I had "pin worms." Now, if I had worms my brothers and sisters had to have had them, too. Every member in the family is at risk if one member of the family has them.

Sweets were a delicacy for us kids. Once, we got hold of some Ex-Lax laxatives that mama had in her purse and ate it all. We thought it was chocolate candy. Needless to say, we were running to the outhouse much of the day!

This time would be the beginning of the end of us, it seemed. Daddy had been a barber, off and on, and landed a job at the Fort Bragg Military Base in Fayetteville. We still had the "Woody," so he had a way to get to and from work and this allowed him to go and come as he pleased.

There was a wonderful black family living next door that had three children: Rudolph, Ruby, and Melvin. Their parents were, as we called them, Uncle Sytes and Aunt Ellen. We would soon find out they were our guardian angels.

Daddy and mama were drinking heavier by this time. We were left alone most of the time to fend for ourselves. I felt like we were better off being left alone rather than to have mama and daddy around fighting. Our sister, Jo, would go babysit for another family and be away from home much of the time.

So many nights we would lay awake, waiting for daddy to come in drunk and waiting for him and mama to begin fighting. I remember the terror I would feel seeing the headlights come into the yard and just waiting for the doors to open and the arguing and fighting to begin.

One night, while Jo was away babysitting, Alice Faye was at home alone with us younger siblings. There was a killer loose in our area. It was announced on the radio and Uncle Sytes' family had told us about it and told us to keep the doors closed and the lights out. We were so frightened that we all gathered in the kitchen and stayed up most of the night because we were too afraid to go to bed and go to sleep. We always thought the worst of things could happen to us. My stomach seemed to always be in a knot, either worrying about something bad happening to mama and daddy; now, to us. Fortunately, I suppose God was watching over us, again.

Another time when mama left, I saw her leave with a man on a motorcycle and it was reported in the local newspaper that she was missing. We were thinking that she was never coming back, or worse, had been murdered; we were always thinking the worst-case scenario.

Daddy would bring a whore to our house when mama would leave. Her name was Dora and she had a young son, Bobby (around six years old). It was close to Christmas and the Salvation Army came out to see what we needed for Christmas. Sonny Boy, Robert, and I said we wanted a bike, since we had never had one. Thank God for the Salvation Army, Fort Bragg Army Base, and the police department! Without them, we would not have had a Christmas!

The police department gave us three bikes: two small tricycles and a larger three-wheeler. The larger three-wheeler was for me because I was the oldest of the three youngest. I was so excited! However, daddy made me give my three-wheeler to Bobby because he didn't get anything for Christmas. I cried and didn't want to do it, but I had no choice. He told me I could share with Sonny Boy.

Bobby was a streetwise kid—no doubt because of the life he had led with his mama being a whore. He must have had to go with her on her many charades. We kids would run behind her singing, *"Knocking down windows, knocking down doors, our daddy is running around with Dora, the whore."*

Bobby was more knowledgeable and more advanced regarding sex than me and my sisters, even though we weren't dummies when it came to sex. When Bobby and his mama would stay over at our house, he would sleep with us and would try to fondle my sisters. I must have been too young, because he never touched me. We felt sorry for Bobby and I've always wondered whatever happened to him and his mama and where they might be, today.

The police report about mama stated, *"She had left home with a sergeant from the Fort Bragg Base and had been gone for three or four weeks before it was found that she was hospitalized in Raleigh, receiving treatment from where he (the soldier) had beaten her."*

After she recuperated, she returned home. She and daddy seemed to be getting along again, no questions asked. I guess they were satisfied with where they both had been and what they had done?

One night, daddy came in late and woke us all up and told us that the "Woody" had burned up. He said that the only thing that could be saved was the front seat. Uncle Ruffin had brought him home, along with the front seat. Daddy brought the seat into the house and it was used for a lounge chair in front of the fireplace that was in one of the bedrooms. We found out later that the "Woody" was going to be repossessed and that they had decided to burn it up to keep the bank from getting it back.

There was an oil burning stove in the living room. We, sometimes, got oranges at Christmas, and mama would lay the peelings on the mantle behind the oil stove to dry until they were crispy. We loved to eat them because no fruit or meat was ever wasted around our house. Our diet mostly consisted of pinto beans and vegetables or whatever came from the fields that surrounded our house.

Just when we thought things couldn't get any worse, things got worse at our house. Daddy began drinking the heaviest ever. He began drinking "white lighting," booze, hair tonic, or anything he could get his hands on.

At night we would sleep with one eye open, always expecting him to come in and wake everyone up ranting and raving. Even if there wasn't anything going on, he would, somehow, make something happen to begin an argument.

Our neighbors, Uncle Sytes and Aunt Ellen, protected us as best they could. Aunt Ellen was bedridden with a disease called MS (multiple sclerosis), and she was very concerned for us children. We spent many hours over at their home because so many times mama and daddy would both leave and not come home.

One of the worst and most memorable times that mama left daddy was when daddy piled all her clothes in the middle of the floor and set them on fire. I still remember seeing the red coat she had worn so many times, burning, and I can still relate to the smell of the burning cloth. Somehow, we managed to put the flames out before any harm was done to the house.

Daddy had been drinking throughout that entire day, and he had been drinking hair tonic! One particular night when he came home, he was acting crazy. He got us all up and out of bed in our underwear, asking us where mama had gone. I guess he didn't have mama there to take his ranting out on, so he took his anger and craziness out on us. He felt we knew where she was and we weren't telling him.

Jo was away babysitting. We were all telling him we didn't know where mama was and he became angry with us and got the gun out and began chasing us around the house, aiming it at us and shooting. We all scattered like a bunch of ants and hid wherever we could find a place. Robert Lee would look for us and pointed us out to daddy when he would find us. Robert Lee thought we were playing the game of hide-and-seek. Since he was the baby, daddy didn't bother him.

Eventually, we all ran in different directions; Alice Faye, Pat and Herman ran in the cornfield behind our house. I ran behind the outhouse and crouched down. I was terrified! I just waited and waited in the cold of the night. I was so cold and felt that someone would find me lying there frozen to death in the morning! My hands and feet were totally numb. My stomach was in knots and I became nauseous. I was afraid to vomit, thinking he would hear me. I wanted to cry but couldn't. I just sat there, frozen with emotions!

I have been wondering when I must have gotten frostbitten on my fingers and toes and believe this must have been the time. I now have Reynaud's disease. My doctors have asked me if I have ever had frostbite because it could possibly be the cause of this disease.

In the early morning hours, daddy went out to use the old outhouse. My breathing seemed loud as I sat hidden behind it. I could hear him in there, mumbling. Thank goodness, he just finished using the toilet and went back into the house.

I remained crouched down there until early morning when I saw Uncle Sytes and Aunt Ellen's lights come on. I ran over to their house and began crying and telling them everything that was happening. They were trying to console me. I didn't know where my brothers and sisters were, and I was so upset and afraid. Soon, Alice Faye, Pat, and Sonny Boy came out of the cornfield and over to Uncle Sytes' house and we were all talking at the same time, trying to explain to them what had happened.

Soon, daddy walked over to their home, thinking we may be there. When he realized we were there, he began yelling at the top of his voice, "Get your asses' home, right now!" Melvin and Uncle Sytes went outside to try to talk to him and try to calm him down, but he wouldn't listen to them. He kept screaming for us to get home!

Alice finally walked out and told him, "We aren't going back home." He grabbed her and began beating her over her head with a military knife (still in its case) and slinging her all around and around. I was screaming to Uncle Sytes, "Kill him. Kill him. He is crazy!" I just wanted him to go away. The feeling I had at that moment is a feeling no child should ever have to feel for their parent. I just wanted him dead, so all the turmoil he caused in our life would end.

Uncle Sytes told Sonny Boy, Pat, and I to get into one of their bedrooms and lock ourselves in and get behind the dresser. We did as he said and waited, not knowing what was happening outside.

Uncle Sytes eventually got through to daddy and calmed him down enough that he released Alice Faye.

Daddy said that if we would go back home he wouldn't chase us anymore and he would stay calm. It took us awhile, but we reluctantly went back to our house. However, before we left to go back home, our guardian angels fed us and calmed us down.

When we returned home, daddy went through the motions of whipping us with the belt, telling us that it was because we ran from him. It was not the typical whippings we were accustomed to, however. He just wanted to show us we had done wrong by running from him. We all kept our distance from him until we felt he had gotten over his rage. We were all walking around the house on eggshells, trying not to make him mad again.

Daddy had gotten over his drunkenness; however, he was still acting a little "crazy," and he pulled his knife out and demanded that Alice Faye cook him breakfast and said he would cut her if she didn't. I don't remember what she cooked, but it must have satisfied him.

Eventually, whatever had made him so crazy wore off and he settled down. We were all still waiting for mama to return.

CHAPTER 11

DADDY WAS HAPPY when mama finally came back home, and as usual, things went okay between them.

During the early morning hours of March 23, 1952, Jo, Alice, and Pat were in their bed, mama and daddy were in their bed, and Robert, Sonny Boy, and I were in our bed.

Sometime in the middle of the night, daddy had become upset with mama and got out of their bed and proceeded to get in bed with Sonny Boy, Robert Lee, and me.

I awoke out of my sleep to the smell of smoke. I ran into the other bedroom to awaken Jo, telling her that I smelled smoke. She got up and we found that daddy had gotten into our bed with a cigarette and the wool army blanket we were covered with was smoldering.

We got a jar full of water from the kitchen and soaked the blanket, took it off the bed, and threw it in the pack room. (The smell of wool burning was sickening to me and I didn't want it on the bed any longer.) We felt the fire was safely out and we went back to bed.

The next morning just before dawn, I awoke to feel daddy picking me up from my bed. He had already picked Sonny Boy up and was holding us both under his arms and was carrying us out of the house. All I could see was flames all around us! He actually threw us off the front porch onto the ground and ran back into the house to awaken the others. When I hit the ground I realized that our house was on fire. As I was getting up I was looking for mama, and I saw her walking around to the other side of the house. I ran after her, yelling for her to come back. She was trying to get in the back door and I kept pulling her by her hand, pleading, "No, mama, no, don't go back in there!" She looked at me and continued pushing on the back door. I kept trying to pull her back and she turned around and said, "I have to get something!" After much pleading from me, and with the fire getting hotter and hotter, she stopped trying to open the door and we both ran back around to the front yard to see if everyone had gotten out.

Daddy had gone back in and had gotten Robert Lee and the other girls up and out. Everyone was saved from the fire! Although, I did go for a long period of time feeling as if there had been someone else in the house who had burned up with the house. (Most likely it was all the memories.)

Daddy kept saying he had lost all his payday money. After the fire, he was out there looking for any coins or dollar bills that may not have burned. I kept repeating over and over that we had lost the bacon that was purchased the previous day. We hardly ever got to eat bacon, which was my very favorite meat. But, the most valuable things that we lost, I feel, were all our photos. To this day, I have never seen any photos of me as a baby. Photos are so sacred to me, now.

It was raining and Uncle Sytes and his family were there to take us in until others could come to help. We were all standing in the rain watching the fire in our underwear. We watched as our home went up in flames; we had lost all our possessions. Since our house was built with wood, it burned very quickly.

The Hubert Huth family from the Fort Bragg Military Base lived a few blocks from us, on Murchison Highway. They came down and took us all back home with them.

Information about the fire was posted in the local newspaper and was announced on the radio. Fort Bragg civilians and the public began sending in clothes, food, furnishings, etc. to help out. Everyone was so helpful. Daddy announced in the paper and on the radio how thankful we were for everyone's assistance.

(Mama and Daddy after the fire)   *(Daddy, Mama, Robert Lee, Sonny Boy, Pat, and me)*

Articles that appeared in the Fayetteville Observer Newspaper:

FORT BRAGG GIs OPEN HEARTS TO FIRE-STRICKEN FAMILY

"When a dawn fire last Sunday made ashes of Mr. and Mrs. Canady's seven-room house on the Murchison Road, they and their six children were left with a lot of problems, little hope and much else.

Furniture, clothing and Canady's weekly pay all were consumed by the flames that flashed through the house in a matter of minutes, leaving the family standing in their nightclothes in a drizzling rain.

But as quickly as the fire brought despair, the actions of a Fort Bragg soldier brought hope and set snow balling a civilian-soldier assistance drive that wrote a happy ending to the story.

SFC Hubert Huth, 3rd Trans. Tuck Co., "Sgt. Bode" Kennel is located 300 yards from the scene of the fire, was awakened by the barking of his dogs at six forty-five, Sunday morning.

"The first thing I heard was the sound of flames crackling," he recalled. "Let me tell you it was a mighty weird sound to hear on the first crack of waking up I looked out the door and saw the Canady house aflame. There didn't seem to be anyone around, but I knew Herman, his wife and their six kids had been home so I jumped into a pair of boots and ran out."

UNCLE SYTES'

When he reached the house, an old cotton farmer named Uncle Sytes was vainly trying to extinguish the mass of flames with bucketfuls of water from a pump 100 yards away. He told Huth that the Canady family was safe in his house and doggedly refused to stop his hopeless attempt at putting the fire out.

As the last flames licked at the gutted structure, the Canady's came out to look at the wreckage of their home.

"It was still raining," said Huth. "The kids were barefoot, cold and hungry. I loaded them up in my station wagon with their mother and father and took them to my house."

While his wife, Louise, was cooking a pot of stew for the wet and hungry brood, Huth placed a call to the home of a friend, Capt. Wilbur griffin, Post Chemical Officer. Griffin's wife, Dorothy, answered the call, and a few minutes later, hair in pin curlers and clad in a house-coat, she walked into the Eutaw Community Church where services were in progress, and told them of the burned-out family's plight. The answer of the community to the call of need had begun.

THE SILVER DOLLAR'

Among the first to knock on Huth's door was Capt. Howard Carey of XVIII Airborne Corps. He went up to the dejected Herman Canady and slipped a silver dollar in his hand. "This isn't to spend," he said. "This one to keep for the luck it's going to bring you!"

Since man can't live by luck alone, Capt. Carey took Canady and his wife to his home while arrangements were made for four of the children to stay with the Huths. The two eldest girls were taken in by a neighbor.

Things happened fast after that. Tiny Martin, announcer for WFNC, told of the family's need in a broadcast, and five minutes later, Sgt Max A. Harker of the Fort Bragg food service school brought a bundle of groceries to the Huth home. Reverend and Mrs. Linder of the Eutaw church began a collection that grew throughout the day.

In the afternoon, an unidentified sergeant who was on orders for the Far East came in to offer the stricken family all his household furni-ture which he had planned to sell before shipping out. Canady's boss at the Mallonnee Village barber shop contacted the owner of the M. W. Smith Moving Company and arranged for a van to make stops at Fayetteville furniture stores to pick up the donations of local merchants.

FUTURE BRIGHTER'

By nightfall, the future palled by smoke in the morning began to look brighter for Mr. and Mrs. Canady and their children, four of whom doubled up with Sgt. Huth's three youngsters for a night of sound sleep.

Monday morning, the Huth dining room was overflowing with clothing and groceries, and cash gifts were coming in via the mail and in person. G.I.'s, Ex-G.I.'s and dyed-in-the-wool civilians all were doing their bit.

"A church took all the young ones downtown Monday and bought shoes for them," Huth recounted. "By afternoon, quarters had been found for the whole family in the Cross Creek Housing Project. There was enough furniture to deck it all out and enough groceries for a month and it looked like clothing to last the year."

"Someone even sent in a radio," said Huth. "Really, it was wonderful the way the people all responded. Please, don't make much of my part. We happened to be on the spot and if we hadn't taken them in I'll bet there would have been a dozen families ready to. It made you glad to be a human being."

HUSBAND GRATEFUL FOR PUBLIC AID

A young barber who, a little more than a week ago, lost his home and all his possessions in a fire on the Murchison road, described himself as a "very lucky man" this morning.

Herman Canady, his wife and their six children barely escaped their burning home, Sunday morning, March 23rd. Only their night clothes, which they wore, were saved.

Today, Canady is settled with his family in an apartment at Cross Creek Court. Neighbors and friends, who heard of their plight, quickly came to the rescue and contributed food, clothing, furniture and money to aid the stricken family.

Canady described himself as a lucky man because no member of the family was injured in the fire. He said that he had tried to thank personally, all who have helped him and his family but has found that impossible so he came to the Fayetteville Observer this morning and asked that the sincere thanks and appreciation of the family be published in the paper

---

CHAPTER 12

AN APARTMENT (in the "projects") closer into Fayetteville, North Carolina, called Cross Creek Court was to be our next home. It was a newer apartment and it was nice because there were many kids to play with. Jo and Alice Faye found friends their age, Pat and I did the same, and there were very young children the same ages as Robert Lee and Sonny Boy. We finally had a place to live where we actually had friends to play with.

There was a swimming pool close by where we would go and watch others swimming and there was a creek close by where Pat and I would go with our friends and swing over the creek on the vines. Sometimes we would be dressed only in our panties.

We had a real bathroom. The first time I tried to use the indoor toilet, I didn't know how. So instead of sitting I would squat, because that's how I had always done. It was great having a place to bathe and having warm running water and a real toilet.

This house even had carpeting in the bedrooms! There were three bedrooms and a bath upstairs and living room and kitchen downstairs. The complex had a row of apartments on each side. A small courtyard was located between each row of apartments.

Once when daddy got drunk he was laying in bed and shot up through the ceiling. He said that he was shooting a fly off the ceiling! It seemed his guns were his toys, especially when he was drunk. His misuse of guns has made me terrified of guns throughout my life.

There was a Holiness church gathering in a tent located close enough by our house that we were able to walk to and from. My mama's family was affiliated with the Holiness church and they believed in Oral Roberts and the tent services. We would go to church and get religion and get all excited and scared to death when they would begin yelling and "speaking in tongues," saying, "The end of the world is coming!"

One night after a tent service, a thunderstorm came up and it began to thunder and lightning. We were so afraid that the end of the world was coming, right then! We began crying and ran all the way home. We had heard just enough about religion that scared us, and not enough to understand it.

This era in our life was short lived. Daddy had begun his heavy drinking, again, and more abuse to mama followed. He was having Dora, the whore, over at times when mama would go away. Once, while Dora was there, she was drunk and she pissed on our new couch. We got so upset with her because it was a nice couch and we had never had a couch before. We just wanted her to go away!

Daddy was also having an affair with a woman he had met at the NCO Club at Fort Bragg. He took us over there a couple of times and I remember seeing the soldiers and women drinking.

I believe that by this time mama had met someone else, too. One morning, daddy tried to get her to do things sexually that she refused to do, and he beat her for it. After daddy left for work, she called us all together and told us she was leaving daddy. She said she couldn't put up with his abuse any longer. She said she would come back for us when she got settled.

We felt mama was leaving for good, this time. She had never called us all together to tell us she was leaving before. I wanted to go with her, but she said I had to stay. I was feeling abandoned by her; however, I wanted her to get away from Daddy so he wouldn't hurt her anymore.

I can still picture her walking away from our house that day. She was wearing a white dress and it was a clear and sunny day. She went to meet someone on the street, who drove her away. For the first time ever, she left without kissing me good-bye! She had always kissed me good-bye when she would leave. I was heartbroken.

Our oldest sister, Jo, was around thirteen years of age (there were six children, from ages four to thirteen). It seems like just yesterday, and that was in 1952. It would be a long time before we would see our mama again.

Daddy kept telling us how much he loved our mama and I believe he did love her. I know their drinking was a big cause of the problem. I also think it was due to the lack of education and their immaturity. The two of them only went to the fifth and eighth grade in school. Daddy quit school to help out on the Canady farm at the old Canady home place.

The following night, after mama left home, daddy came in drunk, keeping Jo up all night to wait on him. Grandpa Jordan must have called the police because an officer came to pick daddy up the next morning and the welfare department had contacted Granny and Grandpa Jordan, in Raleigh, and asked them to come down and care for us until plans could be made for us. Granny and Grandpa Jordan had a Juvenile Court Order of June 26, 1952, for temporary custody.

When daddy was later released from jail he created quite a disturbance in our house, as he did not approve of Granny and Grandpa Jordan being in the house. Grandpa had to take out a warrant on him. Daddy left that night, June 26, and went to Clayton to get Granny Cora and his brother to come get us. The Canady's did not want us to go to the Jordan family, so they decided to take us in.

I never heard what happened to our furniture, and other items given to us from our house fire. I assume that daddy took it all.

CHAPTER 13

GRANNY CORA AND Grandpa Canady's home was such a serene and soothing environment for us. It was nothing like we had been accustomed to. Grandpa Canady owned a community store located on the highway leading from Clayton to Pythian Home. Grandpa Canady walked with a limp in his left leg. He would walk to and from work each day and we would wait in anticipation for the bag of candy he would bring us when he came home. He was a man of few words, but when he spoke, you would listen and you better have listened well.

(Front row: me, Sonny Boy, Robert Lee, and Granny Cora;
Back row: Pat, Alice Faye, and Jo)

Their home was a five-room home, with a bathroom. It had a front porch with a swing and rocking chair. The home was located on Page Street, in Clayton, North Carolina. Our Uncle Gene and Aunt Nellie lived next door. We had had very little contact with the Canady family, and this was an opportunity to get to know them better.

Granny Cora fed us a lot of banana sandwiches spread with mayonnaise and smashed up bananas, sometimes with peanut butter. By adding mayonnaise and sugar to the bananas, it would make it go further to feed us.

There was an oil heater in one room that heated the entire one half of the home. However, across the hallway there were two bedrooms with no heat. At night, Granny Cora would tuck us in her big feather bed in the cold bedroom and put warm towels on our feet. It was really cold when we first got into bed, but it was wonderfully soft and warm in a matter of minutes. We felt so safe and secure at Granny Cora's home.

(Granny and Grandpa Canady's home)

(Granny Cora and Grandpa Canady)

There were a couple of families living close by that had children the same ages as my brothers and me. We would go over to their homes to play; the family that lived across the street and the family living two houses down.

Once, while we were swinging on the porch swing at the home across the street, I was pushing my brothers on the swing and it swung back and knocked me down on the porch and I blacked out. They took me back over to Granny Cora's and she told me to go lay down. I went to sleep and slept for hours. When I awoke I had amnesia for a day. I couldn't remember what had happened and I didn't even remember when I had come to live with Granny Cora. Eventually, my memory came back and I seemed okay. Nowadays, I suppose they would have called it a concussion.

Granny had chickens in cages in her back yard and she would go out and wring their necks (sometimes she would chop their heads off) and cook them for dinner. We would laugh, seeing them run around and flop around with their heads cut off! Granny Cora would tell us, "You kids run around like chickens with their heads cut off!" Fried chicken would taste wonderful to us. We always had good food at Granny and Grandpa Canady's house. She was a good cook and you would never leave her table or house hungry.

Granny also had a little shed out back where she would make her lye soap for washing clothes. It had a dirt floor. Me and my brothers and some of the neighbor's kids would make a playhouse out of the shed and play hospital. We pretended we were doctors and nurses, checking out each other's bodies. Like I've said before, we kids were not dumb when it came to the "birds and the bees!"

We were at Granny Cora's house only a couple of weeks before it became too much of a burden on her and we were all separated and sent to live among our aunts and uncles, with exception of Sonny Boy and Robert Lee. They remained with Granny Cora and Grandpa Canady. Granny Cora was always especially close to Robert Lee. She always said he reminded her of daddy, when daddy was a little boy.

Jo went to live with Uncle Battle and Aunt Violet, Alice Faye went to Uncle Winston and Aunt Janie, Pat went to Uncle Ruffin and Aunt Ailene, and I went to live with Aunt Cora Lee and Uncle Bill.

I suppose there were a few prayers said for us from our grandparents: "God please save us from these kids." I felt we were a burden on them, all along. We would overhear their conversations when they would all get together, saying how much of a burden we were on them.

Many of the Canady family members were farmers in the Clayton area. We would try to help out in the tobacco fields while we were living with our aunts and uncles. I remember me and my cousins would rub tobacco leaves in our hands to make it look like we were working harder than we really were. We learned how to pick and top tobacco and we would pick the large leaves from the stalk and learned how to string it up and cure it in the tobacco barns.

Those tobacco worms were the ugliest and the largest worms I had ever seen! They were green and looked like they had horns on their head and seemed to have a thousand legs. We would pick them off and mash them on the ground. The juice that came out of them looked like wet chewing tobacco! We would also help pick cotton and help bundle it up to go to the cotton gin.

Aunt Cora Lee and Uncle Bill lived in the old Canady home place, where Aunt Cora Lee was born.

(Old Canady Home place [then])

(Old Canady Home Place later...it has since been demolished)

Aunt Cora Lee had three children: Dorothy, Thomas, and Rosa Lee. Rosa Lee was more my age and it was nice having Rosa Lee for a playmate.

(Aunt Cora Lee with Me and Rosa Lee)

Rosa Lee and I would play in the fields and make mud pies and loved to watch the farmers on their tractors and turbines. One of their neighbors' boys got his arm caught in the turbine and lost his arm. That's when we discovered that farm equipment was dangerous and that we should stay away from it.

Aunt Cora Lee milked the cow and made butter in a churn. Rosa Lee and I would use our fingers to lick the cream off the top of the churn. They had an old smokehouse where they would hang meat to cure.

This home had an outhouse, too. But, it didn't seem to matter to me at the time because I felt I had a family again!

Aunt Cora Lee also sewed beautifully. She made Rosa Lee and me dresses out of flour gunnysacks. It was amazing what pretty dresses came from an old flour sack. Rosa Lee and I were about the same size, so Aunt Cora Lee could use the same patterns when sewing. We dressed like twins at times.

I loved Aunt Cora Lee and Uncle Bill. She was like a mother to me. Uncle Bill was a quiet man and worked in the fields. I never heard him raise his voice to Aunt Cora Lee or the children.

Dorothy had a boyfriend named Van and she was like an older sister. Thomas was like my older brother and he was very handsome. I was very happy and content living with them. I felt safe and could sleep all night long without turmoil in the home. Rosa Lee and I had fun playing and running around the yard with our games. I suppose I taught her a few games to play, too.

(Me [left] with Rosa Lee)

I felt as if I finally had a normal family. I was happy at Aunt Cora Lee and Uncle Bill's home.

One of our kittens (my favorite little white kitten) became missing and we wondered what had happened to it. Several days later our well water began having little white hairs in the water. We had a man come out to check the well, and there was my missing kitty. I cried and cried for my little friend.

We couldn't drink the water for several days until the water was filtered. After this had happened, they closed the opening to the well to protect anything from getting into it. I missed standing up on the side of it, looking into the dark, deep waters, wondering how it would feel to jump into it—but remembering that I wouldn't be able to get out! It was fun to look down there and see your reflection in the water, so far below. I had many nightmares about falling into wells, since we seemed to always have abandoned wells around our houses.

I spent approximately nine months with Aunt Cora Lee and Uncle Bill. Even though they had three children, they treated me as if I was one of their own.

Then, one day, they came to tell me that I was leaving to go live somewhere else. I began to feel abandoned again. Granny Cora and the preacher at the Baptist church in Clayton, North Carolina, had found a Baptist orphanage, Mills Home Baptist Orphanage, in Thomasville, North Carolina, that would take us in.

In November of 1952 I received a psychological examination to see if I qualified for Mills Home. The results read, *"This attractive and friendly child took her test in a serious manner and tried hard and intelligently without showing any over degree of tension. She earned a mental age score of eight years, nine months, which is well within the normal rage for her age. She has a slight speech defect in that she substitutes W's for R's in most words. She should be able to make normal progress through school, and her undesirable speech habit should be subject to correction without great difficulty."*

In December of 1952, Granny Cora and the pastor at their church, Rev. Hoqwell, sent a request to the Smithfield DPW (Department of Public Works), asking that we children be placed in the Baptist orphanage. They had tried to get us into Kennedy Home, thinking it would be closer to our relatives. They were planning to send me and my two brothers to Kennedy Home (or if the two boys weren't of age, they would go to Mills Home until they began school), then, they would be transferred to Kennedy Home. It was finally decided to send us all to Mills Home, to keep us together. Alice Faye and Pat almost did not get accepted into Mills Home due to Alice Faye's age and Pat's emotional state.

Pat felt that she had been bullied while she was living with Uncle Ruffin and his family, by his children. She was unhappy there and Uncle Ruffin refused to allow her to stay with them through the summer months, because he had been told that it would only be on a temporary basis.

Pat was the only one of us who was in school while staying at Uncle Ruffin's home. All the rest of us were not attending school. Social services confronted Granny Cora about us not being in school, and she stated it was most likely because of the expense of the book fees, etc.

Reported from the social service files: *"Mrs. Canady (Granny Cora) stated that it nearly broke her heart when Herman married Hazel. She said Hazel and her family were of lower moral standard, had no scruples against doing anything, and that Mr. Jordan forced*

Herman to marry Hazel. That is all Mrs. Canady was able to say, but Mr. Eugene Canady said that his brother was forced to marry Hazel because of his own "sorry doings" and that he had never assumed his responsibility as husband and father. He stated he had drunk excessively and had been very cruel to his wife and had in general made no effort to hold his home together. He stated that both the mother and father knew this but were unable to say so. He blames his brother more for the breakup of the home than he does his sister-in-law, as Alice Faye had said earlier, that the children's mother had never learned to cook and was not a good housekeeper, but that she first began drinking with her husband. He stated that Mrs. Canady often had bruises where her husband beat her while drunk. He said the children were equally as fond of their mother as their father and they blame one as much as the other for the breakup of the home. He said that the children were exposed to most of the conflict in the home. He, too, said that the father would never contribute to the children's support until the court forced him to do so. He believed that an agreement without the backing of the court would be of little value.

He said further that he and his brothers and sisters could not take the children. There has already been some family friction regarding the children in that all of them knew their father is eager to be rid of his responsibility. He said further that the children's father had promised to help support the children while they were in his parent's home, but he only did so when the family threatened to bring a suit against him and then only in a very small amount."

On January 6, 1953, the social worker sat us all down to explain to us where we were going and what to expect when we arrived there. She felt we understood and we all said we didn't have any further questions about it. She wrote that I told her, *"I don't care where I live, just so long as I get a home where folks love me!"*

We were living with our aunts and uncles from June 1952 until February 1953, prior to being placed in the orphanage.

CHAPTER 14

ON FEBRUARY 9, 1953, Uncle Ruffin gathered us all up to go on our journey to the orphanage. My oldest sister, Jo, was too old (they wouldn't take anyone over the age of thirteen). She was almost fourteen years of age at that time. Alice Faye was twelve, Pat was ten, I was nine, Herman (Sonny Boy) was seven, and Robert Lee was five years old when we all were sent to live at Mills Home Baptist Orphanage (the name was changed to Baptist Children's Home, later in the 1950s).

This place that we would be calling "home" was founded in November of 1885 by John H. Mills. Mary Presson was the first child to entered Mills Home, along with her mother, who was the first matron of the home.

Sonny Boy had decided he didn't want to be called "Sonny Boy" any longer and wanted us to refer to him as "Herman." It was hard changing over, but everyone began calling him "Herman."

We had been abandoned many times before, but I had never felt the abandonment as strong as I did that day heading to Mills Home in Thomasville, North Carolina. Thomasville was more than one hundred miles from Clayton, North Carolina. Sitting in the back seat of Uncle Ruffin's car, I cried all the way to the orphanage. Words can't explain then sadness, loneliness, and aching feelings I felt that day.

All I could hear on the way to the orphanage was the turning of the car's wheels and Uncle Ruffin talking (it sounded like words all scrambled together). He tried to talk to us and tried to cheer us up, but there wasn't much response from us. It was one of the saddest days of my life and it was one of the most frightening, not knowing what to expect in this strange place. I felt so abandoned and unloved!

(Entrance to Mills Home Orphanage - Girls side)

(Entrance to Boys-side)

The orphanage's campus was shaped like a horseshoe with arches on each side. All the girls were located on the left side of the campus and the boys were located on the right side of the campus.

When we arrived, Uncle Ruffin dropped us off at the infirmary. We went there to be checked out for any diseases, lice, worms, etc. We had every bad-tasting medicine you can think of and many shots given to us during our stay there, which was almost a week. We were not accustomed to being tied down and restricted from being out-doors, and my little brother, Robert Lee, continually ran all over the infirmary and gave the nurse, Miss Lee, a hard time by climbing up the curtains. She was always trying to tame him down.

(Infirmary)

After being de-wormed, checked out, and given the appropriate shots, we were sent back to our prospective cottages, to meet our matron (housemother) and the other girls and boys.

*(Me, my brothers, my cousins Thomas, and Rosa Lee
at Mills Home's old swimming pool.)*

(Witty Cottage)

Alice went to live at the Witty Cottage and everyone was calling her Alice, instead of Alice Faye.

(Herman was sent to live at the Simmons Cottage prior to being moved to the Chowan Cottage.)

(Simmons Cottage)

(Chowan Cottage Boys
[Herman1st on 5th row])

Robert Lee went to the Miles Durham Cottage that had one of the sweetest and best housemothers on the campus.

(Miss Hoyle, housemother at Miles Durham Cottage)

(Robert Lee with his Miles Durham brothers and sisters Cottage [Robert Lee top right])

("Big Girls" at Miles Durham)

All the young children had "big girls" to help them with their meals, bathing, clothing, etc.

As we grew older, we would be moved to another cottage to be with our own age group. This would continue until we graduated from high school.

(The Valley/Playground)

There was a large playground area called "the Valley," located between the two sides of the campus. There was a merry-go-round in the valley that we all called the "Ocean Wave," and that was the biggest attraction in the valley. I got my nose broken, once, while I was walking and talking to someone. Not paying attention, I walked right into it while it was full of kids, going very high and fast!

(Ocean Wave)

(Slides/Ocean Wave/Baseball Field)

(Mitchell Cottage)

Pat and I were sent to live at the Mitchell Cottage. There were sixteen girls in this cottage. Pat and I were put in separate bedrooms, but we had a "Jack and Jill" (adjoining bathroom) between our rooms.

I handled my emotions pretty well until my brothers and sisters and I were separated. Many nights I would go to bed crying, feeling so alone and wondering if I would ever have someone to really love and care for me. As a child, you feel like you are the cause of your parents splitting up and your being abandoned. I suppose all the many times that mama and daddy left home and stayed away had taken its toll on me.

I would hold my feelings inside as if nothing bothered me and would make sure that I always cried alone. I did this for so long that no one expected me to cry. I believe they thought my feelings couldn't be hurt. At one minute I would want to cry; the next minute I would be laughing. I felt as if I had a split personality. I would stand in front of the mirror, smiling, trying to find a look that I could hide my emotions. . . while inside I was always hurting.

At the Mitchell Cottage, Miss Tingley, our housemother, was a strict matron. A lot of the girls did not like her. However, she did show

Pat and me some attention in that she taught us to play cards. She enjoyed playing with us, and many evenings, after study hall, we would play Rook and Rummy card games with her.

(Miss Ella Tingley, matron at the Mitchell Cottage [1953])

Miss Tingley would not allow us to watch TV, except what she wanted to see. She would watch the soap operas, such as, *Search for Tomorrow* and *The Guiding Light*. She also liked to watch *Ed Sullivan*, and other entertainment shows. When the cowboy shows came on, she would shut the TV off and say, "You are not going to watch those shoot 'em up, bang, bang, movies!"

Another one of her famous sayings was, "Who do you think you are, John D. Rockefeller?" (In the 1950s, the Rockefeller family was one of the wealthiest families in the America.)

At times, Miss Tingley would walk all sixteen girls uptown to the Davidson Theater to see a movie on Saturdays. The movie tickets were only twenty-five cents.

(Davidson Theater - Thomasville)

On one particular Saturday, she took us to see the movie, *"Miss Sadie Thompson,"* starring Rita Hayworth. The movie was a little risqué in those days for children. Miss Tingley didn't realize it until we were in there and immediately told us to all get up and leave the theater because we weren't going to watch this "dirty" movie. So, all sixteen girls had to get up and march out of the theater. We were so embarrassed but giggling as we exited the theater.

She would have a day off each week, and most of the times when she would return from her day off I would have to go in to see her for something that I had done wrong during her absence. "When the cat's away, the mice will play," as they say.

Once, when I was at church attending GAs (Girls Auxiliary), another girl dared me to jump out the church window. Give me a dare and I would do it! I jumped out the window and Miss Tingley heard about it and she punished me by making me sit on the toilet in her bathroom for hours, after bedtime. I would drift off to sleep and almost fall off the toilet.

Pat and I worked in the kitchen and we were always horsing around with each other every chance we would get. Once, I pulled the rug out from under her feet and she fell and hit her chin on the corner of the table and blood began gushing everywhere. I was terrified that I had hurt her badly and would also be punished for it. However, we both made it appear as if it were an accident. WHEW!

Pat and I would fight at times, too. That's when our favorite saying would come out, "I hate you and wish you were dead!" Sometimes, I would look at her with mixed feelings, with a little twinge of jealousy. I thought she was so pretty. But, later, I came to realize that a sister is like a mirror; she was reflecting back to me the best of who I was.

There was an abandoned railroad track right behind our cottage and we would climb down the hill to the tracks and pick the pretty pink, wild roses. While picking flowers one day, I thought I heard a rattlesnake's rattle. I leaped down off the hillside and stabbed her with the scissors. Now, this time it was an accident! Thankfully, it only glazed her arm and it wasn't a deep cut.

(Me and Pat, age ten and eleven)

We had many good times playing with all the other girls. We would play hopscotch and jump rope like we had always played at home. But, there were sad times, too. There was an "Ocean Wave" (merry go round) in the yard and we would sit on it and sing a song that made us all cry. It went like this: *"I'm a poor little orphan girl, my mama she is dead. My father is a drunker, won't buy me no corn bread. Home, home, sweet home; home, home, sweet home. If I were an angel, I'd fly to her grave. I'd stay there forever, and never go away. Home, home, sweet home; home, home, sweet home!"*

(Ocean Wave at the Mitchell Cottage)

There was an old swimming pool on the girl's side of the campus. This was one of the few times I had ever been able to swim in a clear-water pool. We were more familiar with murky swamps, creeks, rivers, and lakes that never looked so clear and blue, like the color of the sky. This pool was where the children were baptized while the new church was being built.

(Old Swimming Pool)

The administrators at Mills Home seemed to want the children baptized into the Baptist Church as soon as they felt that we understood what baptism meant. We would have to talk with the preacher, and if he felt we were ready, we would be baptized. (Of course, Granny Jordan's family had taught us a lot about the Bible since they were involved in the Holiness Church.) I was baptized when I was ten years old, in the old swimming pool, where I also learned to swim. I don't believe I would have ever learned to swim if it had not been for the clear water. I was afraid to go in any water where I couldn't see the bottom, because of my fear of snakes.

Once, while I was swimming, one of the younger girls came up to me, trying to play with me in the pool. She continually kept hanging on me and trying to tease me. It began to annoy me so bad that

I dragged her into the deep part and pushed her off me, knowing she did not know how to swim. She was going under for the second time when I realized she might drown if I didn't help her. I pulled her back to the shallow part where she was safe. She finally stopped pestering me.

Eventually, the swimming pool closed and we had a brand new pool. It was much larger, with two diving boards. One was a really high diving board and I was afraid to climb up it, afraid of heights.

(New Swimming Pool in the Valley)

The lifeguard, a stocky, heavy set girl, told me that she would climb up the ladder on the high dive with me and we could hold hands and jump off, together. I felt safe with her being a lifeguard. We climbed up there and slowly walked to the end and I stood there, frozen. With a little coaching, she convinced me to jump. Needless to say, upon jumping with my small, 70 pound physique, she hit the water first and dragged me into the water, face first! The pain was terrible but I was so embarrassed that I wouldn't show the pain to the other swimmers. I never again got back on the high dive!

We had swings at our cottage and Pat and I, with our southern accent, would say, "Yunguns, will you come push me?" We called them "Yunguns," and they would laugh at us because of the way we talked and acted. Looking back, I suppose we seemed very "backward" to them.

I would never get close to any of the girls because I didn't trust them and didn't want to get hurt, thinking they would turn on me, someday.

Baptist churches around North Carolina would supply us with clothing and sometimes we would get identical clothing to wear. Once, we all got identical raincoats. When we would go to church, we would all have to walk down the church aisle wearing the same kind and color of raincoat. It was so embarrassing; although, we were always excited to get new clothes.

(Rainy day girls—1955 Mitchell Cottage girls
[Me 1st on 2nd row/Pat 2nd on 3rd row])

When the boys on the campus would misbehave, they would have to dig up tree stumps around the campus. It would take days to get the job finished. We always knew who had misbehaved when we would see who was digging up stumps.

Each girl had duties for a one-month period of time: cleaning the bathrooms, sweeping, mopping, kitchen duties, and shining the floors. We would wax the floors with a mop and then get down on blankets and shine the floors by crawling around on them. We would chase each other around on the blankets. Of course, Miss Tingley would not allow it and would scold us for it.

There were two "big girls" living in our cottage, who would help us with our homework, comb our hair, and help us get dressed, like big sisters. Sometimes, they were nice, but other times, they were not very nice to us younger girls.

Once, one of them, obviously in a bad mood, said to me, "You think you are something, don't you? But you aren't!" It hurt my feelings so bad. I went to my room and cried. I would always make sure I was alone when I cried, so no one would see me. Of all the girls in that cottage, I was the least one to feel that I was special! I was very insecure and felt intimidated by some of the other girls. I was smaller than most of them and was very homesick for my brothers and sisters. I always felt a little different and felt like no one loved or cared about me!

One of the milk truck drivers, an older boy, would bring milk and tease me saying things like he loved me and would wait for me when I grew up, etc. I would run and hide every time I saw him driving up. I have to admit I enjoyed the attention but it was embarrassing to me to have the other girls hear him talking. I knew he was just kidding, all along. Pat knew about it and watched out for me by letting me know when he was coming around.

The first school I attended while at Mills Home was Liberty Drive School, when I was in the fourth grade. It was very close to Valentine's Day (the day before), and when the valentines were given out I didn't get a single Valentine. I felt rejected; even though I realized no one really knew me at that time, it still made me feel rejected. The teacher felt bad for me and gave me a valentine!

I always loved it when Easter would come around at Mills Home! We would always receive a fancy dress and shoes, along with hats and gloves to match, from our "clothing people" to wear to church on Easter Sunday. "Clothing people" were either private families or churches that would pick kids' out to furnish clothing to.

(A typical go-to-church/ Easter Sunday)

I was always proud when Mother's Day would come around, because I would get to wear a red rose, showing all the other kids that my mama was still alive! There were so many children there who did not have a living mother and had to wear a white rose. This made me feel more special, wearing my red rose.

When I was in the fifth grade, my teacher, Miss Clara Harrison, called my name to come forward. I didn't recognize it because she called for "Joy" to come forward. I just sat there as she was looking at me. Since my name was "Jerrie," I had no reason to respond. She called "Joy" again— no response. Then, she came over to my desk and said, "Is your name Joy?" I said, "No, my name is 'Joy'." The class laughed out loud. She thought I was trying to be funny, but with my speech impediment, I was trying to say "Jerrie" and it sounded like I was saying "Joy." My eyes became watery, but I didn't cry.

It was the end of the day when Miss Harrison told me to stay after school. After talking with me, she realized I wasn't trying to be funny and apologized for embarrassing me in front of the class. In the meantime, I had missed the school bus back to the orphanage. By my being so shy, I didn't want to tell her I had missed the bus, so I walked all the way back to the orphanage, through town, alone. Miss Tingley was upset with me for not telling someone that I had missed the school bus.

Later, Miss Harrison and I became buddies. She would invite me over to her home after school (of course, after getting it approved with my matron). Maybe she just felt sorry for me? She lived in a really nice brick house and I enjoyed going over to visit her. She would ask for Pat to come along with me, at times because she sensed I felt uneasy getting any special attention.

Also, when I was in the fifth grade, I was in a school talent show and dressed up as a Holland girl. I wore my little wooden shoes and sang: *"I'm a little Dutch girl Dressed in blue, here are the things I like to do: salute to the captain, bow to the queen, turn my back on the submarine. I can do the tap dance; I can do the splits. I can do the holka polka, just like this."*

(My fifth grade school photo)

I moved from the Mitchell Cottage to the Biggs Cottage with Imogene Wilson as my matron. We had two "Big Girls" staying there with us. One of the girls would call me in her room to comb my hair and hug/kiss me saying, "I love you so much." I felt weird having another girl telling me she loved me. I looked up to her and thought it was okay. I never did know how to take a compliment, but wondered why she loved me. She was a pretty, well known "big girl" around campus and I respected her a great deal.

It was during the time that Hurricane Hazel hit North Carolina. All our window and doors had to be boarded up. That was very scary time for us all.

Around this time, a group of experimental medical group came in and did all kinds of tests on us. They had us strip down to our underwear and measured us, weighed us, took strands of our hair, nail samples, etc. for an experiment. Later they came back and did it all over again in a couple of weeks, to see results. We never heard any results or figured out what the heck they were there for. I suppose they were using us for "guinea pigs" for some experiment.

We always had to take the big blue school bus to school.

(On our way to school)

We had only one bad accident on this big blue bus. It was in 1957.

REBECCA JACOBS   MICHAEL McDONALD

(Article from Charity & Children Newspaper)

It was in the Baptist Hospital—Room 424—Rebecca Jacobs and Room 511—Michael MacDonald, the place where two young bodies quietly lay. There had been a terrible accident on the way back from school. The bus driver, Paul Edinger, had no idea what was about to happen on the road ahead and did not see the protruding iron bar. The iron bar stuck out like a lance onto the road from a double decker auto transport carrier. It happened in a flash as the iron bar speared through the metal of the bus and leaving much pain in its wake...

The doctor diagnosed Rebecca with a depressed brain concussion, a broken arm, a broken leg, and deep flesh wounds on her leg. Michael, who lay in Room 511, was also in much pain, with two broken legs.

Every child at Mills Home felt the pain when terrible things would happen to any of us.

At this time in my life, I felt I wanted to be an actress. My girlfriend, Betty Jean, and I sang in a talent show at Liberty Drive School. We sang, *"How much is that doggie in the window; the one with the ugly face. How much is that doggie in the window? I do believe her name is Sian, not Grace. I must take a trip to California, and leave my poor sweetheart alone. If he has a doggie to protect him, then the doggie will have a good home. How much is that doggy in the window? The one with the wiggly tail; how much is that doggy in the window? I do hope that doggie's for sale."*

My seventh grade teacher, Miss Evelyn Brandon, soon married and her last name changed to Hunt. She was a really nice teacher and she also seemed to take a special interest in the children from the orphanage. She was a small-framed, petite, and lovely lady. She was young at heart. All the students liked her.

(My seventh grade school photo)

Once, when we were standing to say the Pledge of Allegiance in our classroom, I backed up to a heater/radiator and burned the back of my leg and knee. It was so painful, and when I looked down at it there were blisters popping up on my leg. I was so embarrassed to have anyone notice, so I went all the rest of the day hurting and I wouldn't tell anyone about it. When I got back to the orphanage after school, I showed it to my matron and she insisted that I go to the infirmary to have it tended to before infection set in. She was upset that I had gone all day with my leg being so badly burned and so shy and embarrassed to mention it to my teacher.

In the eighth grade, I went from elementary school to junior high at Thomasville High School, on Main Street. I was excited to go to the high school, but really felt intimidated. I was embarrassed having to ride the blue bus to school. I was voted as the secretary of my eighth grade class and felt it an honor. I was also a pretty good artist and was asked several times to draw on the bulletin boards, particularly maps.

Intimidation finally got the best of me. I began backing off from taking part in any activities in my class. The kids from the orphanage couldn't stay after school for extracurricular functions like the "uptown" kids could do. We had to catch the bus and get back to the orphanage immediately after school let out. I felt jealous of the uptown girls who were able to participate as cheerleaders, majorettes, etc. None of the girls from the orphanage could get involved with any of those activities.

I always looked forward to Sundays coming around at Mills Home, because that was the day when we could visit with our brothers and sisters and get together on the campus to talk, laugh, and cry. It was so enjoyable to be able to connect with them. The only other times, during the winter months, that we could see each other would be on Friday nights and Saturdays at the Gymnasium and the Valley.

During the summer months, we were very busy with activities of all sorts all around the campus: swimming, softball, basketball, Church activities, skating, tennis, etc. (Of course, our duties had to be completed, first.) The Valley would be open every night after supper until 9 p.m., except for Sundays and Wednesdays when we would need to attend church.

Every girl had duties to do around the campus: kitchen duty, sewing room, infirmary, laundry room and print shop. Older girls had to go to the younger girls' and boys' cottages, as "big girls," to prepare their meals and help bathe and dress them for church, school, etc. This meant getting up very early in the mornings before heading out to school.

The boys had to manage the farm and dairy. The boys would have to do the hard work, such as milking the cows and working in the fields. The girls would also have to pick beans and peel apples and peaches. We even raised our own chickens on the farm and would have to clean them and cut them up prior to cooking. By cleaning the chickens we had to gut them, pluck them, burn the hairs off and cut them up prior to frying them. (I am willing to bet not too many girls this age could do this or be willing to do it.)

Hay Haulin' Time

The older boys would drive the milk truck and food truck, delivering to each of the cottages.

We got salaries for our duties. Much of the time it would be twenty-five cents a month. We had rules to abide by, and if those rules were broken we would be put on punishment by not being able to watch TV, go to the valley or not receive our salary.

While living with sixteen other girls, we had to learn to get along with each other real fast! We also learned to take care of ourselves. If other girls felt they could, they would tease you and bully you. Sometimes, they could get really mean. Being so small in stature, I always wanted to prove to them that I wasn't a "pushover." It was the same way in the boys' cottages—one of the boys was burned by having cigarettes put out on him and he was bullied until he finally left the orphanage. I'm sure there were other things that went on that we never heard about.

I never liked conflict, so, I would stay to myself quite a bit. By my not trusting others made it harder to make close friends. I kept my feelings bottled up inside and I was very selective in allowing anyone to get close to me. I made sure no one knew my thoughts and my feelings. I carried a lot of resentment and anger within me and it showed at times, I'm sure.

I signed up for the Mills Home basketball team (before Mills Home teamed up with Thomasville High's team). I was the smallest girl on the basketball team. I did pretty well for what I had to work with. I would shoot the goal over my head so it would make it harder to be guarded. When I shot, my whole body would come up off the floor. At one of the games I scored quite a few points and it felt so good to be recognized. A teammate came up to me and said, "If you keep that up, you will be an excellent player someday." That really felt good to get praised for something I did!

(Mills Home's basketball team [I am third from left; front row])

When we joined up with Thomasville High School basketball team, I gave up basketball. My insecurities made me give up a lot of things in high school. I felt that I was becoming my own worst enemy!

We had a basketball court and a tennis court (on dirt) next to our cottage. We would all gather to play basketball. I remember, once, while playing, I was guarding a girl who was a large Indian girl by the name of Shirley. I was guarding her too close and she began to bang me on the top of my head. Since I was much shorter than her, she had no problem landing hits on top of my head. I was frightened that she might knock me out, so all I could think of was to kick her on her shin as hard as I could with my black and white oxford shoes. I was amazed when she released my arm and stopped hitting me! I've always thought she acted like a bulldog (hit them on the nose and they release anything they have hold of).

As you can see, below, we soon became friends after that incident.

(Shirley, Betty Jean, and Jerrie)

The cottages were old (some older than others), however, we always had clean, white, ironed linens on our beds and it was not unusual to see a big black cockroach crawl across our beds. We would just swipe it off and go on sleeping. We had to make our beds up each morning, just as soon as we got out of bed. If the beds weren't made up perfectly, the beds would be ripped up and we would be put on punishment.

(Girls from the Downing Cottage)

I was only at the Downing Cottage for a short period of time, because I and my matron did not get along. Once, prior to going to school she came into my room and said something to me that I did not like and I said something back to her and she lifted her hand to hit me and I said, "I dare you, go ahead and see what happens to you!" She walked out. When I returned from school that day I was told I would be moved to the WC Cottage.

Since each girl had chores to do in her cottage, nothing could ever be out of place. The housemother would take a broom and sweep out from under our beds (to see if there were anything thrown under them). We knew we had to keep our room spick-and-span, at all times.

We had chords, but we always managed to kid around and chase each other around, tease, and wrestle with each other.

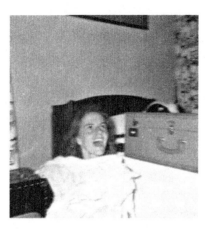

(Me playing around while packing to leave for a vacation)

The caseworkers from social services stated in our case reports that they felt the Canady children would be "forgotten children" once we went into the orphanage. She was right; I certainly felt that way, too. It was quite a while before we heard from our daddy or any other family members after we were admitted to the orphanage. All we had was each other to cling on to.

Daddy had been asked by the social worker if he would allow adoption of the children if it became necessary, since sometimes children do not adjust to an institution life. Daddy told her that he was in agreement with us being adopted, should the issue arise.

Daddy also told the social worker: *Mama had left home for the first time in 1945 in the company of a man. This was shortly after she began drinking. She returned in about two weeks and told daddy she had gone to visit her mama in Raleigh. He said that after he returned from service she began leaving more frequently and began staying away for longer periods of time. Daddy said she left on several occasions, leaving us without food and uncared for and never considered our welfare and this continued until she left for good.*

Our case reports also showed that daddy had told them that mama had left home several times with men. He never did admit that his actions may have played a big part in her leavings. Even though we never saw any of them, nor heard about any of them, daddy accused her of having several affairs with different men. He said mama never gave any consideration for us children. However, it seemed to us that he was the one who was having affairs—even bringing one home with him, a few times.

When daddy finally came to visit us, he was with a woman who had seven children! We later found out that it was the same woman my sister, Jo, had babysat for while we lived in Fayetteville.

(Martha, our stepmother)

(Daddy and Martha)

They began coming to take us out for vacations in the summer and at Christmas. Each time I would go on vacation with them I would come back nervous, upset, moody, etc. I would get called over to see my caseworker for counseling due to my mood changes.

Daddy and Martha would argue, cuss at each other, and fight, just like he and mama had always done. Her children were living in the same atmosphere that we had to live in when we were living with mama and daddy. They would begin drinking, and sooner or later they would start yelling and cussing at each other and that would lead them to fighting. I would always be happy to get back to the orphanage.

Once, while we were on vacation, daddy was driving the car very fast while he was intoxicated. I was sitting in the back seat behind him and I was so nervous and afraid that he was going to crash. I was hitting on the back of his seat, saying, "Daddy, slow down. Please slow down." He reached back and hit me on top of my head. It hurt so bad I thought I was going to pass out. It made me so angry I just sat back and kept quiet, not even caring at that point if he did crash.

In my early tweens, while I was visiting with Daddy and Martha, after he had been out drinking, I woke up to find him in my bed, snuggled up to me with his hands on by breasts. I was so embarrassed, even though I had not begun to develop yet. I did not know whether to jump up out of bed or quietly and slowly slide out. I decided I didn't want to wake him up, so I slid out of bed as quietly as possible without awakening him. I never mentioned it to anyone, because I felt he was too drunk to know where he was and what he was doing.

My sisters and I were upset with him and blamed him for our being in the orphanage, and to know that he was raising another woman's seven kids!

When we first met Martha, she had on a fur coat; it really upset us, because mama never had anything that nice to wear and the little she did have, he destroyed!

He never paid one cent to the orphanage to help in their raising us. In the contract between him, Granny Cora, and the orphanage, he had promised to pay $40 a month to Mills Home! He couldn't pay $40 a month, but he could raise someone else's kids and send them to school? He even paid for one of them to go to barber school!

Alice was even more upset with him in the way he treated Martha, compared to the way he treated mama. Alice never got along with her. I wouldn't allow her to get close to me, either. Martha tried to be nice to me, but I never accepted her as a stepmother, knowing the past history.

(Daddy and Martha)

We met all of Martha's children when we would go on vacation and we liked them a lot. We felt closer to the oldest of her children, Everette, Ned, Geneva, Sylvia, and Joanne, because they were more our ages. They had a dysfunctional family life, also. Everette was like our big brother, and to this day, he attends our family reunions. We had fun with all of them going to Buckroe Beach when daddy and Martha lived in Williamsburg, Virginia.

(Martha with six of her seven children)

In my early teens, I had a little "crush" on Ned (one of Martha's sons). Martha had good-looking children. Ned was so handsome and we went to the movies together, once, with one of my cousins, Jimmy, and Ned's sister, Sylvia. During the movie, Ned told me he was going to the restroom. When he returned, I realized that I was missing my purse which had been lying between us in the seat. I never found it, and to this day I feel he took my purse when he went into the restroom. Needless to say, that cured my "crush" on him.

Later, we were told that Ned was killed while he was living in Texas; Geneva and Joanne have since passed away, but Everette and Sylvia are still living in North Carolina. Martha also had two other boys whom I have never met, and they are also living in North Carolina.

(Robert Lee, Herman, Joanne [Martha's daughter], Pat, Me and Alice)

(Alice, Pat, Me, Herman, and Robert Lee)

While we were swimming at Buckroe Beach, Jo was swept into deeper waters and she didn't know how to swim. She had stepped into a hole and the water was up around her neck. She began to panic and I got behind her and pushed her toward the shoreline until she could walk out of the water. She never liked going near the water and she never learned to swim.

My brothers and sisters and I bonded many years ago and I feel that is what has pulled us through "thick and thin" over the years.

Each child living in the orphanage was assigned a caseworker who would call us in their office and try to get us to open up with our feelings/emotions, etc. But I would just sit there and not say a word when they tried to get me to talk. I didn't trust anyone. My caseworker at that time was Mr. Ball. He realized that I had a real problem opening up, so my case was turned over to Mr. Allred. He was able to get me to open up more and it became more apparent that my vacations with daddy and Martha were causing me stress and emotional anxiety.

Mr. Allred knew of a family in Chapel Hill, North Carolina, who wanted to take one of the children from Mills Home back home with them for weekends. Their names were Mr. and Mrs. Billy Williams. They were nice and I remember attending church with them and meeting some of their relatives at a get-together. I only visited with them a couple of times and Pat went with me, once, to visit them. One sad day, Mr. Allred informed me that Mr. Williams had committed suicide. I felt so sad for their family.

Very few members in the Canady or Jordan family came to visit us, except for daddy, Granny Cora and our sister, Jo. They would come to visit once in a while on Sundays. A typical Sunday afternoon visit would be gathering together in the Valley.

Jo remained at Granny Cora's home, where she went through school and graduated from Clayton High School. After she graduated from high school she went to live with daddy and his new wife, Martha, in Virginia.

(Jo in high school)   *(Jo at sixteen years old)*   *(Jo's senior high school)*

(Alice, Me, Robert, Herman, Pat, Jo, and Granny Cora)

(Pat, Me, Jo, and Alice at Mills Home)

(Pat, Me, Jo, and Alice in the Valley)

(Herman and Robert Lee in the Valley, on the "Ocean Wave")

Alice was getting involved with activities at the orphanage: cheer-leading, choir, etc. She had also acquired many friends. She was very outgoing and made many friends.

(Alice on the swings in the Valley)

(Alice [far right] as a cheerleader at Mills Home)

(Alice [first row, far right] with her basketball team at Mills Home)

Alice tried to adjust to Mills Home's rules and regulations, but it was hard for her living in that strict environment. She became friends with many of the other girls. One girl in particular, Eleanor Johnson, became very close to her. We all referred to her as our sister because we loved her so much. One of our saddest days came when we heard that her little brother, Ronnie, had been killed by the train. Eleanor and her brother had entered the orphanage in August, 1952, while our family had arrived in February, 1953.

We felt as if we had lost a member of our own family and gathered together with her to grieve. Eleanor is still considered a member of our family. She remains in touch and attends our family reunions now.

(Alice and Eleanor at Mills Home)

(Eleanor with us at our family reunion)

(Alice and Eleanor)

Ronnie Johnson

Article Written in the "Charity and Children" (Mills Home Newspaper, 1954)

"A pre-Christmas tragedy which took the life of one of the children cast a blanket of sadness and gloom, over the Mills Home campus.

On Friday afternoon, December 17, the day before the children were to leave for the holidays, Ronnie Johnson, eleven-year-old Green Cottage youngster and a friend, Woodrow Shields, thirteen, from the Mother's Cottage, were on their way to town to do a bit of last-minute Christmas shopping. Excitedly talking about what they planned to buy with the money clutched in their hands, they were unaware that a southbound 176-car freight train was almost on them. Woodrow saw the oncoming diesel in time to jump out of the way, but Ronnie apparently froze in his tracks.

An ambulance was called, but it had to go several blocks down the tracks before it could cross. In the meantime, life in Ronnie's body was ebbing away. He lived only forty-five minutes, passing away at the Thomasville Memorial Hospital of a fractured skull.

-Stunned, Deeply Grieved-

News of his death spread quickly over the campus. Children and staff members alike were stunned and deeply grieved. It was hard to believe that a happy, smiling boy like Ronnie was gone. But he was. The Christmas party, always the climaxing yuletide event at Mills Home, was cancelled. In the cottages that night what conversations there was centered on the tragedy.

The next day, Saturday, General Superintendent and Mrs. Reed went to Ronnie's hometown of Valdese, North Carolina, to help make the funeral arrangements. The child's mother died nearly three years ago and his nearest family contact was his maternal grandparents.

A sister, Eleanor, age fourteen, is a resident of the West Chowan Cottage at Mills Home. The two of them came to Mills Home in August, 1952.

Friends stood with bared heads in the icy winds, at his funeral. Among those present was his father. One of the Christmas presents Ronnie had planned to buy with the dollar and half he had in his hands when he was killed was for his father.

Although two Mills Home staff members have been killed at the tracks, Ronnie was the first child. Dr. M. L. Kesler was killed in 1932 and Miss Alice Rudd, a teacher in the Mills Home School, met her death in 1926. It had been more than twelve years since a death had occurred among the children at Mills Home.

Among those most deeply hurt by Ronnie's death was Mrs. Mae Belle Doughton, his cottage mother. "He was such a good boy,' she said after the funeral. 'At night when we had our prayers, he always asked God to make better boys out of the Green Cottage boys. We will miss him so much.' And so will everyone else at Mills Home."

Mills Home has a private cemetery (God's acre) in the woods behind the campus where some of the children from the orphanage who had died with the Black Plague many years ago had been buried. However, some of the workers and children have been buried there throughout the years. We would take long hikes through the woods and go visit the cemetery to read the tombstones. We always felt sadness during our visits there because it was so run down.

Some alumnae and alumnus have gotten together and built an entrance to 'God's Acre' and cleaned it up and now it appears more kept. It is no longer a place of gloom and doom but a peaceful place where one can celebrate life and speak of loved ones who have passed on.

(God's Acre-Cemetery)

Another one of our brothers from the orphanage was killed in a car accident in 1957. This article was published in the "Charity & Children" newspaper:

1957

(James McGee)

<u>James McGee</u>....*his death is mourned by Mills Home family.*

"*Tragedy struck Mills Home campus with the death of sixteen-year-old James McGee from the Watson Cottage. The lights of a 1940 Ford instantly went out on the car and for James. Lights out, the car skidded in a curve and tumbled twenty-five feet down into a creek. The car was driven by Jerry Clontz, a former Mills Home student. James came to live at Mills Home in September, 1952. He leaves two sisters, Jane and Helen.*

Another sad occasion was when one of Robert Lee's best friends, Jerry Thomas, was hit and killed by the train that runs through Thomasville. This article appeared in the "Charity Children" newspaper from one of our workers:

"A Scrap of Brown Paper Highly Treasured"

"*It is only a small piece of brown wrapping paper, torn on one side and smudged in the corner. But, it is not for sale.*

For it tells a story—of a skinny youngster who rang my doorbell one hot day a few weeks ago. It was a late Saturday afternoon and the carnival was in town. Many of the Mills Home youngsters had gone, but this lad said he didn't want to go.

Then the carnival bug got hold of him and bit him hard, like most boys, when they get to thinking about it, and he decided he just had

---

to go. But, he didn't have any money.

He stood there on my front porch, first on one foot and then on the other. He eyed me timidly and straightened to say his piece. "They got five rides that I have just got to ride at the carnival, but I don't have any money and they cost a quarter a piece. Can you loan me a dollar and a quarter?"

It was all out in one breath and he volunteered to write a note as I dug into my wallet.

In a few minutes a beaming youngster bounced down my steps and darted through the Mills Home arch, carnival bound, while I held the scrap of paper and looked at the scrawled letters: "I.O.U. . ."

I hope he enjoyed the carnival, for while neither of us had any way of knowing it at the time, it was to be his last one. A few days later he was killed on the railroad tracks by a passing train and that's why my wrinkled piece of paper saying, "I.O.U. . . $1.25—Jerry Thomas," is not for sale.

By: John E. Roberts

(Jerry Thomas)

Sadness struck again for all the Mills Home family in 1966:

(Sherry Yow)

Chair City Senior Killed in Wreck
April 8, 1966
"To live in hearts we leave behind is not to die."

THOMASVILLE – A Thomasville Senior High School student was killed, and her boyfriend injured, yesterday near Asheville when their car skidded on wet pavement and struck an oncoming vehicle head-on.

Miss Sherry Elaine Yow, 18, died at 1:50 p.m. at an Asheville Hospital following a two-car collision on U.S. 70 in Swannanoa. The driver of the car, Garnett McDonald Cumbo, Jr., also of Thomasville, suffered slight injuries, but returned home.

Cumbo was released under $1,000 bond pending the outcome of an inquest at 10 a.m. today in Asheville.

Mrs. Garnet Cumbo Sr., mother of the youth driving the death vehicle, said the two high school seniors were en route to Western Carolina College for a weekend campus visit. Both had been accepted by the college and were to enroll there next September.

Miss Yow was a resident of Mills Home, and had lived there since 1957.

She was born in Lexington on Feb. 5, 1948, a daughter of George Ernest and Ella Octavia Ward Yow. She had lived with her parents until entering Mills Home.

The funeral will be held at the Mills Home Baptist Church Monday at 4 p.m. by the pastor Rev. Roger Williams. The body will remain at J.C. Green and Sons Funeral Home until placed in the church 30 minutes prior to the service.

The family will be at the funeral home Sunday from 7 to 9 p.m. Place of the burial will be announced later.

Alice could not adjust to the way of life at the Whitty Cottage. The matron there was once employed at a detention home for girls and that's the way she ran the Whitty Cottage. She would strike the girls with a belt and was very strict with them. We also learned that she would catch stray cats and burn them up in the barrel outside that was used for burning trash. She was a short, fat woman and looked the part of a mean prison guard.

Once, on a Sunday afternoon, Alice called us all together and told us she had heard from our Aunt Johnnie, and that mama was in a sanatorium in Baltimore, Maryland. She had contracted tuberculosis. That was the first time we had known where she was since she left home. Alice had a photo of mama, in bed, weighing only sixty-nine pounds! We cried just seeing her photo and how bad she looked.

In May, 1956, Alice also told us that she was going to leave the orphanage to live with Aunt Johnnie and Uncle Bert. I was heartbroken, thinking she was leaving us all alone. She was our only contact with the outside world, it seemed.

Later, we were told that she had no choice in leaving Mills Home. She wasn't adjusting to the rules of Mills Home, and they had insisted that she leave.

Aunt Johnnie was concerned that it would really have an effect on Pat, but I think I was the one it affected the most. I was really hurt at the time and didn't really understand how she could leave us there.

She had been our "big sister" ever since we had arrived. I cried a lot when she left.

She was good about staying in touch with us, however, after she left.

Aunt Johnnie would come and take us on vacation at times, after Alice went to live with her. Aunt Johnnie had two sons, Bert Jr., and Bobby. They were about the same ages as Pat and I. We would play games with them and fish at a nearby pond in Wilson Mills, where they lived.

Alice had a boyfriend who would come over to visit and sometimes bring his buddies and they would sit and talk and drink at times. Once, her boyfriend asked me if I had ever kissed a boy and I said no, and he grabbed me and kissed me quickly and it seemed my face was wet all over! I would stay clear of him from then on!

I was in my teens before we were able to see mama again. We took a bus trip up to Baltimore, Maryland, to visit with her at Aunt Billie's house. She had been given visiting rights from Mt. Wilson Sanatorium to see us and I was afraid to hug mama or be close to her because of the fear of contracting tuberculosis.

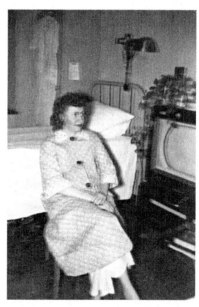

(Mama at Mt. Wilson Sanatorium in Maryland)

She was soon released from the sanatorium in Maryland and was transferred to a sanatorium in Raleigh, North Carolina, for further treatment.

She had gained a lot of her weight back and looked much better than she did in the previous photo that we had seen. She lost one of her lungs during her bout with tuberculosis and she had begun dipping snuff to loosen the phlegm in her remaining lung.

(Robert, Mama and Herman)

(Jo, Mama and Pat)

(Mama and Me)

It was a happy time for all of us to finally be able to see our mama! Alice was now living in California, with Aunt Johnnie and her family. She did, however, come out via train to be with us in Baltimore.

(Jo and Mama in Baltimore, Maryland)

Robert Lee wasn't adjusting to Mills Home life, either and had tried to run away a few times. He was a mischievous little boy and kept things going on all the time in his cottage—nothing major, though. He was a bright little boy and could do much better in the classroom than he attempted to do. Eventually, his case worker suggested that he be sent home to live with daddy and Martha.

After living with them for a few years, he was not doing well in school, so he quit school and lied about his age so he could join the Service. He joined the navy and was stationed in Pensacola, Florida, serving four years. During his time in the navy, he formed a band and was the lead singer. They referred to him as "Bob," but he lost the name of "Bob" quickly after he got out of service. (He will always be Robert to family.)

(Robert Lee,
fifteen years old)   *(Robert Lee, school photo)*   *(Robert Lee, navy photo)*

Pat, Herman, and I were the only members of our family left at the orphanage. Pat and I would go for long periods of time before we would get together on Sundays. I always felt that she liked her girlfriends more than she did me. But, later in life, I found out she felt the same way about me. We were so close to the same age, I suppose there was sibling rivalry between us.

I still seemed to carry a grudge and had a lot of anger. On the weekends, after all my chores were completed, I would lie on my bed and listen to the radio and write my inner feelings down on paper. I would make certain no one else would see what I had written because I would write it backwards (mirror writing), then I would tear it up. Thank goodness for my caseworker—I needed him!

In December of 1959, written in my caseworker's file: *"Jerrie Canady has been a special project for some months now and I have had regular interviews with her for some period of time. Jerrie is a very difficult child to talk with and is subjected to moods that last for days at a time. It took me a good deal of time to get to know her very well and have her rely on me and trust me. I discovered that she has been most affected by her parents behavior prior to her coming here and she is very sensitive about her family and their behavior. Jerrie is an intelligent child and very loveable, once this barrier is broken through. She has needed awfully bad some family to relate to."*

(Jerrie, thirteen years old)

One Sunday, during visiting hours, Pat came to see me, crying. She had received a letter from mama stating that mama felt that she loved Martha more than she did her. Pat was so upset! I tried to calm her down and spent a long time with her, talking. She felt so sad that she had made mama feel that way. I felt closer to Pat than I had for a long time. I was glad to be there for her.

Pat was a beautiful girl with beautiful red hair. She was also a cheerleader at Mills Home.

(Pat with Herman and Robert Lee at Mills Home) *(Pat's senior photo)*

(Pat cheerleading at Mills Home)

(Pat, Nineteen years old)

(Article written by Charity & Children Newspaper)

GIRL OF THE WEEK

(Pat Canady)

"Patricia Canady, 18 years of age, entered Mills Home from Clayton, North Carolina, 1953. She has spent seven years here on the campus growing up. Her life in the different cottages was normal, some little problems always getting in the way but being overcome with commonsense and help of others. Pat feels that the problems solved are the growing part of "growing up." She is most grateful for the chance of living that part of her life here. She feels that God has a purpose for her life and that she has received her basis training at Mills Home.

Mills Home has offered so many things that are outstanding that Pat couldn't choose any one big thing as being outstanding in her memory of living here. The little things are what count in her life, for every day some little thing happens or is accomplished that makes living more enjoyable. She chose one little thing that has been a blessing to her, and that was singing in the sextet. She has also enjoyed her past four months in the work program, and this has been with the little boys at the Simmons Nursery. Pat has a job waiting for her in Greensboro and she will begin work June 6th. Beyond this, she has no plans but will count the little things or problems as progress toward maturing into womanhood.

This odd quotation from Pat answers concerning her stay at Mills Home: "In asking me to express my feelings about a place I have called home for the past seven years is like asking me how I would feel knowing I am drawing my last breath." I said odd and I shouldn't have. I can go back in memory and a feeling similar to what Pat said. She expresses her gratitude to so many people who have made her take a plan and a purpose for. She expresses her training in these words, "I want to make my life a life that will reflect God's purpose for me." – C. Franklin Bailey

(Pat's graduation class, 1960 [Pat in center, first row])

When she graduated from high school in 1960, it left only me and Herman remaining at Mills Home from our family.

I always acted and try to appear older than I really was, but I had never kissed a boy. I felt insecure and awkward thinking about a "boy and girl" relationship. I began wearing three-inch high heel shoes at the age of thirteen years old! Some of the other girls would tease me and tell me that I looked like Minnie Mouse in those shoes!

Being so skinny and wanting to look like some of the other maturing girls, I would stuff my bra and underwear to fill me out to look more mature. I was so self-conscious of being so skinny and undeveloped and was even taking pills called; "Weight On," to gain weight. Pat would provide the pills for me when I would visit her in Greensboro.

(Jerrie, sixteen years old)

I was beginning to become attracted to boys, however. One of my girl friends was also becoming attracted to boys and we decided to practice kissing each other so we would know how to kiss a boy and to have a little experience in kissing. We would kiss each other goodnight and any other time when we had a chance; we were best friends. We, both, were going through an awkward age and experimenting.

Once, I had a boyfriend who tried to get me to meet him in a clump of bushes when I had finished my duties helping the smaller children with their supper. He said he would meet me there when I got off duty. I didn't want to meet him, so I took another way back to my cottage to avoid him entirely. I also avoided him from then on. This was always my way of breaking up with someone. I would just avoid them entirely and they never understood why. I had already seen so much in my life that I felt kissing was bad and sex was dirty. Never could understand how preachers could have children, did they really have sex?

Being as shy as I was, I had a crush on a boy mostly through high school, but never let it be known. I did have a couple of "boyfriends" throughout high school. But, having a boyfriend at the orphanage was like having them walk you home after church, seeing them at church, or sitting with them at the *Valley*. It seemed I was always interested in boys older than myself.

We always looked forward to our boyfriends walking us home from church (especially in the evening). We had many large oak trees which shaded us during the daylight hours and shielded us in the moonlight hours.

It was rumored around the campus that one of our male house parents would hide up in the trees to watch to see if any romantic couple would stop to steal a kiss or two. Some of the boys on campus caught him, one night in a tree, and began bombing him with acorns.

When I was in the eighth grade, my boyfriend was a senior in high school. I felt he was too immature for me. When we would listen to Elvis' songs at the teenage center at the gymnasium, he would sing along and move his body like Elvis. I thought he was being too silly, so I just stopped speaking to him and ignored him when he would come around; my way of "breaking up" again.

Since I was such a late bloomer growing up, and having to live with fourteen to sixteen other girls, I learned that girls grow up so differently and they mature at different ages. All the girls in my cottage had their periods (menstruation), most of them by the ages of twelve or thirteen. I was the only girl who had not begun my period in my cottage and thought there was something wrong with me. I would go into the bathroom and pretend I had already started, going through the motion of changing and cleaning up, just as the other girls were doing. Then, one day while on vacation, I was sitting on the sofa at daddy and Martha's house with my legs up on the sofa and daddy walked into the room and pointed at me and said, "Go take care of things." I had no idea what he was talking about until I suddenly looked down, and I had begun my period. I was almost sixteen years old!

(My ninth grade photo)

My sister, Jo, had met a handsome sailor named Jim! She was so proud to be seen with him and seemed to be so in love! They were married in South Carolina (no marriage license was needed in South Carolina). Following their wedding they moved to Virginia and had a baby girl named Cindy. We were so happy for her, knowing she had found true love.

In 1960, mama went to live with Jo and her husband in Raleigh, North Carolina, after she was released from the sanatorium. I would go visit them, at times.

Once, while I was visiting, mama had been on a date and when she returned, she was drunk. She and I were sleeping together in the same bed. I remember saying to her, "Mama, why do you drink? I wish you wouldn't drink." She said, "It helps me to forget things." I cried myself to sleep that night.

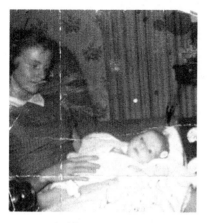
(Me holding my niece, Cindy)

(Mama holding Cindy)

(Mama after her release from sanatorium)

Jim, Jo's husband, turned out to be sorry excuse for a husband; he was such a womanizer. Alice told us that once, while she had been sleeping with the two of them, he had tried to reach over the top of Jo to get to her, trying to fondle her! He would beat up on Jo and things continue to get worse between them and they eventually divorced. He has since passed away.

Jo met a really nice man, after her divorce from Jim. His name was Carl and she fell in love again. They were married and lived in Alexandria, Virginia, where she became pregnant with her second child. They named her Carla after her dad. A few years later, she became pregnant, again, with a son, named Eric. They had a lovely home in the suburbs of Alexandria and seemed to be very happy. We were so happy for her. She deserved much happiness!

(Jo and Carl)

Once she found a baby snake in her basement, it frightened her so that she insisted they move to another home in the area. She thought that if there was a baby snake in the house there had to be a mama snake somewhere, close by! Eventually, they moved into another home and later moved to the Delaware coast.

Since I was always upset when I returned from vacations with daddy, my caseworker found a family who was looking for a girl to take out on vacations. They were also looking for a girl to adopt, since they had two sons. They were a nice family from Durham, North Carolina. They were from an upscale family. He was a girl's basketball coach at the high school.

They were the nicest family and I loved them. When I would kiddingly call her "Mama," she would tear up and say, "I wish you were my daughter!" They loved me, too. It felt so good to be loved! I felt that I was finally getting the caring and loving that I had always needed.

She made me an outfit for Easter one year and I was so proud of it. They would take me out of the orphanage often on the holidays. Since I had been baptized, I felt really good going to church with them. I became very close to their entire family.

She would correct my speech, at times, because I had terrible language. I'm sure, if I had been adopted by this family, I would have gone to college and would have been a debutante, or such. They seemed to be the perfect family.

I became friends with the preacher's daughter, and, once, we went to see the movie "South Pacific," and then went out with some of her other friends for pizza. This was the first time I had ever tasted a pizza! I felt as if I was a member of a very special family!

Since their desire was to have a girl in their family, they checked into adopting me from the orphanage. However, I was told that my daddy would not sign the papers for my adoption, even though he had told the caseworker that he would agree to an adoption if the time arose.

They eventually ended up adopting another girl from another agency. However, we stayed in touch for many years afterward. I never met their new daughter and always felt jealous of her. I always felt she was a very lucky girl!

I was moved to the WC Building when I turned sixteen.

(Mae Arnder [matron])

(WC Cottage)

Mrs. Arnder's son was visiting, and he was a photographer by trade. He wanted to take photos of us diving into the water at the pool and I proceeded to dive in. I had a swimsuit that tied around my neck and when I hit the water the strap broke and my swim suit slipped all the way down to my waist! When I came up he was just looking at me, smiling. I was so humiliated by what had taken place that I was too ashamed to look at him and stayed clear of him when he would come for visits, thereafter.

One night when I walked home from church with my boyfriend's little brother, my matron, Miss Arnder, called me into her room and said, "I'm sick and tired of you and your boyfriends." I said, "He is not my boyfriend, he is just a friend and he is my boyfriend's little brother." She didn't seem to believe me. I didn't understand at the time, but, looking back she was in her forties and I think she must have had a hard time growing older or, was she jealous?

She would wash and style my hair at times and that made me feel a little weird (getting the attention other girls weren't getting). She would also lay out in the sun with me on the WC building rooftop. The roof is where we would lay to get our suntans because with the roof being tin, it allowed the sun to reflect more. We would use baby oil mixed with iodine to tan . . . seemed it worked at getting us a better tan.

CHAPTER 15

ONE DAY I was walking across the orphanage campus and a boy on campus came running toward me. He was attempting to make it look like he was going to run into me. I jumped to one side and he jumped the same direction and literally knocked me off my feet onto the ground. I jumped up screaming at him, "You idiot, why did you do that?" I was furious and he just looked at me, apologizing as best he could. I just left him standing there. He continually approached me to tell me how sorry he was that he had knocked me down. I finally accepted his apology and also was beginning to think he was a very nice guy.

There was a "Junior Youth Week" at the Mills Home Baptist Church, where everyone elected a new group to take care of business in the church for the entire week. The boy who had run into me (Paul) was elected the pastor of the church and I was elected the secretary. He had to give the sermon the following Sunday, and he did a wonderful job.

(Youth Week Officials-1960[Me and Paul bottom right])

Paul was handsome, a real gentleman, and wore a crew-cut hair-style. I began noticing Paul more and more and then we became a couple and it continued all though our high school senior year. We went to the senior prom together. In my senior year of school, I went home on vacation and when I returned, he had bought me an engagement ring. We were known as high school "sweethearts" at THS (Thomasville High School). The school posted a full-page photo of me and him on the front pages in our yearbook.

(Paul and Jerrie, high school yearbook)

(Paul in the Valley)   *(Paul's Senior Photo)*

Paul was athletic, playing basketball and baseball on the Mills Home team (before Mills Home and Thomasville High combined teams). He was being "scouted" by a local Greensboro team and had dreams of one day playing for the Brooklyn Dodgers!

(Paul played basketball)   *(Paul played baseball-bottom left)*

We had always heard of Johnny Allen, who once played for the New York Yankees. He was a Mills Home alumnus and would come back to Mills Home at times to visit with the children. All the kids were proud and looked up to him because of his connection to Mills Home. Now, they have a Johnny Allen Scholarship Award presented to a child from Mills Home each year.

Paul's brother, Larry ("R" is what everyone called him), almost drowned in our new swimming pool. They were having a swimming meet with different events. This particular event was to see who could stay under water the longest. "R" went down and somehow became stuck on the stair ladder. Everyone else had come up and we were waiting for him to surface. The lifeguard finally went in after him and he was lifeless. They quickly performed CPR, prior to calling the ambulance.

I ran across the Valley and found someone who would go to the boy's Watson Cottage to get Paul. Paul came running just in time to ride to the hospital with him in the ambulance. It was very scary for all of us watching. We were so happy to find out that he would be okay.

Paul's younger brother, Cecil, was the cutest little boy! He would gather other kids around at the valley and he would sing and wiggle his hips to the song Elvis made famous, "Hound dog."

Paul's other brother, Raymond, was a good-looking blonde with blue eyes. I always felt really close to Raymond. He was always so nice to me and friendly. Everyone seemed to like him a lot.

Paul's mother, Isabelle, was a sweet lady who would come visit her boys at Mills Home. Sometimes when she would visit, I would visit with them down at the Valley. She once told Paul, "You better always treat her well." He did, for sure. She was a lovely lady. We became very close.

Paul had a close friend named JD who was tall and stout in stature.

(JD Combs)

They would walk together uptown and Paul would buy me banana milkshakes. JD, being so tall, could hand it up to me through my bedroom window. Fresh banana milkshakes were always my favorite! I would always refer to JD as a "gentle giant". He had such a sweet personality.

I roomed with my girl friend, Barbara, and we would play tennis on the courts next door. We played against sisters who were known to be very good tennis players and we eventually beat them! We were so happy to be able to say we had beaten those two because they felt they were the best!

Barbara had a boyfriend named Jimmy, who was really handsome, and they made such a good-looking couple. He had given her a gold necklace, and once, while she and I were playing around in our room, I was pretending to break her necklace and I accidentally broke it! I felt so bad and she became so angry with me. I apologized, but she was too angry and wouldn't accept my apology. It hurt me so bad, but she eventually forgave me after I fixed it for her. I seemed to always be joking and playing around with my friends.

I was so upset when I found out that she was leaving Mills Home to go back home. She was such a good friend and I hated to see her go—and our tennis game was on a roll and we needed to beat those sisters again! Again, I felt I was losing someone else that I loved.

As she was getting into the car, she looked up and saw me standing in the upstairs window, crying. She ran back inside and hugged me good-bye. I wept for a long time, thinking that everyone I had ever cared for seemed to leave me! I've never seen or heard anything from her since that day.

I would wrestle and tease some of the girls and there was another girl by the name of Barbara. Once we were wrestling and I began choking her, and geez, all of a sudden, I realized I was choking her too hard. I stopped and decided I was not going to wrestle like that anymore. I realized that wrestling with my brothers was different than wrestling with these girls.

When I was a senior in high school, a scientist came to our high school to present a science show and his lady assistant became ill. He picked me out of the audience to fill in for his assistant during the show. He made my hair stand straight up with electricity running through my body and I began performing in a way that made all the students laugh. The more they laughed, the more I performed! He really liked me and told me I could become a good actress.

When the show was over and we had gone back to our classroom,

I was called into the principal's office. When I arrived the scientist was standing there. He told me that, after I graduated from high school, he would like to send me to Mars Hill College to major in acting. He thought I had good potential for acting. He took my name and gave me his telephone number to contact him after graduation. I was excited just thinking about it and the potential of an acting career.

I had always dreamed of being an actress and thought this would be my big chance. At times, I would stand in front of the mirror and pretend to act and sing. I was so excited that I would have an opportunity to attend college and major in acting.

When I told Paul about it, he said, "Oh heck, that guy just wants to get in your pants." I disagreed with him, saying I didn't think that was the case. But, eventually, after much discussion I was convinced and there went my chance because I never contacted the scientist again.

Being that I had such a desire to be an actress, I signed up for dramatics class in high school. I, once, pantomimed to the song, "Tall Paul," recorded by Annette Funicello. (I always heard that she and Paul Ankle was a couple and the song was written for him.) *"Everyone knows that I love Paul; Tall Paul, Tall Paul, he's my all."* Others in dramatics thought it was funny since Paul and I made such a cute couple and he wasn't tall, at all!

Our dating at the orphanage consisted of Paul walking over to my cottage and us sitting in the living room, along with other couples, and the matron would sit outside the room looking through the glass doors. There was a large mirror on the wall and she would sit and look at us through the mirror. Usually, there were two or three couples sitting in the living room together.

After mama left Jo's home, she went to live with Granny Jordan until she met a man named Leo. She would always sign my cards, *"Love Always, Mama and Leo."* (I still have in my possession every card mama sent me while I was at the orphanage.)

Mama and Leo were never married. Their relationship did not last too long. She soon met another man named Bill Payne. They were married (I think) and lived in Virginia. I never heard whether or not my daddy and mama ever really got divorced; never saw a marriage license from either of them with their new partners, either.

Pat and I went to visit mama and Bill on vacation, once. He wasn't very nice to my mama, either. One night, Pat and I overheard her crying in the night. We didn't know what was going on, but we listened and wondered and it sure made me dislike this guy.

(Mama and Bill Payne)

Bill went to prison for reasons we never knew. Mama went back to live with Granny Jordan in Selma, North Carolina. She never saw Bill again and none of us ever heard anything more from him and that was okay with us.

(Mama with Herman and Robert Lee)

It was wonderful that Herman and Robert Lee had the opportunity to spend more time with mama, since they were so young when she left home.

(Mama and Daddy at Granny Jordan's)

Mama, Daddy, and Martha had always remained friends. Mama would go visit with them at times. There was no jealousy shown among them. Sometimes when she would visit, it would be during the time we would be there on vacation.

Mama stayed in touch with us and many times, we would go visit her. She remained with Granny Jordan until one day in January, 1961, when she became ill with a cold that turned into pneumonia. Granny Jordan told us that mama woke up in the middle of the night and couldn't breathe. Granny tried to help her, but had decided she better call the ambulance. Mama was frightened and kept saying, "I don't want to die. I want to see my babies again!" Mama only had one lung left after losing one during her bout with tuberculosis. Her remaining lung collapsed on the way to the hospital in the ambulance and she passed away.

That evening, during homework study time at my cottage, I received a phone call from Martha asking, "Is someone there with you?" I said, "Yes, my matron is here." She told me to get my matron close by and then she told me that my mama was dead. That's all I heard her say. I just handed the phone to my matron because I was in shock and unable to talk to her. But, deep inside, I didn't like the idea of her being the one to call to tell me that my mama had passed! Why didn't my Daddy, or Granny Jordan, or anybody else call me?

Mama died on January 16, 1961. She was buried on January 18, 1961. The service was held at the funeral home in Selma, North Carolina, and burial was at Selma Cemetery. She was only thirty-nine years old. All I could think of at the funeral was that she had had such a hard life for the small amount of years she had on earth. We all still resent her name on her tombstone being "Payne" instead of "Canady."

My caseworker at this time was Mr. Quinn. He was a wonderful man. I became very close to him and his wife, Barbee, and their son, Timothy. Mr. Quinn's mother had died when he was only a toddler and his father died when he was thirteen years old. Being orphaned at such a young age, he felt he could relate to the kids at Mills Home. He not only could, he did.

Mr. Quinn drove Paul, Herman, and me to the funeral. Alice Faye was in California and couldn't attend the funeral. Daddy, Martha,

Robert Lee and Jo came down from Virginia, and Pat was there, too. This was such a sad time for us all.

I remember seeing daddy leaning down and kissing mama on the lips. I always knew he still loved her until the day she died. They just weren't able to live together, peacefully.

I have a small gesture that I do at the funerals of loved ones; I pull a strand of hair from my head and place it in theirs. This is like taking a part of me with them. It just makes me feel better to do this and it seems to help with the closure.

The day after my mama's funeral, I sat down and began writing my feelings out on paper—as I was so accustomed to doing. This time it wasn't written backwards.

Written January 19, 1961:
Dearest Mother,

I know it's to late for me to write to you . . . I know you can still read it, so I'm going to write to tell you how I really feel about you. I've never been able to let you know how much I really loved you. You know I love you. I know we couldn't live together like other mothers and daughters, but no matter what happens you will always be my mother.

I know you have done some things you have regrets for. . . daddy has too, but I'll love you and daddy until the day I go and be with you. I know you are happy! At least, you won't have to suffer anymore. You, being our mother, help God take care of us all.

Alice is doing fine, so don't worry about her. She loves you just as much as we do.

I never thought I would live to see you the way I saw you, yesterday (January 18th). It hurt me so bad. . . after seeing how happy you looked, it calmed me down. Because, then, I knew you were in a safe place. I could see you looking at me, while I was looking down upon you lying there. You were the prettiest and sweetest mother in the world!

I'm so glad you were ready to die. If you weren't it would hurt me the rest of my life. I hope to see you in heaven some day.

I hope you could see all of us, yesterday, because that was your last wish. I would give anything if we could have been with you when you went to live with the Lord. I know he is taking good care of you. Now, you can see Alice Faye, and know she is all right. I'm sure she would have loved to have seen you. She was living so far away. You never did get to see her children. They, and mine, will always know you because I will never let them forget you.

I'll have to go now. . .

I've come back to complete my letter to you. I hope you can see and know what I am writing to you. I know you know how I feel.

Mother, you may be gone from this earth, but you will never leave me as long as I live. You will always be in my heart as the dearest mother on earth!

I wish you had been able to meet Paul before you left us (that was one of your wishes, too). You told us not to marry until we were twenty and then you wanted to meet the man we married (Pat and me). I want you to know they (Wiley and Paul) were at your funeral. Did you see them? I hope you saw them because they are the boys Pat and I will marry. Mama, since you told us not to marry until we were twenty, will you forgive me if I married before then? I'm sure of myself and him. I know you will understand; you have always been so interested in who I went with.

Did you see daddy yesterday, too? He was so hurt. I know he still loves you and I know you still love him, don't you? I wish so much I could have been with you and talked with you all of my seventeen years.

I only wish you and daddy could have lived together. I know you suffered plenty. I witnessed some of it. . . some, I didn't. We all will suffer before our death, but you didn't deserve all you got. Everybody fell in love with you. . . your personality. I wish I had inherited it. I've been told I look a lot like you (I'm glad). I wish I acted like you.

Mama, I may not show it, at times, but when you died a part of me died. No one knows but me how much died.

I want you to know I still love you with all of my heart!

Mama, tell God I'm not blaming him for taking you away from us. He has blessed us in so many ways. Remember four years ago when you were in the sanatorium when you asked God to let you *see us again. He did for four years! I'm so grateful for it. I really never thought I would see you again after you left home that day.*

You never realized it, but the day you left, you didn't kiss me good-bye. . . it hurt my feelings so bad. (You always had me spoiled by kissing me every time you would go out the door.)

Also, do you remember in Raleigh, when you, Pat, and I used to tease you about being a "teenage mama?" I will never forget us laughing at that and many other things we shared together.

Mama, please don't think I held it against you because you drank. The only reason I felt you did was that you wanted to forget, just for a little while, the hardships you had to live with. I don't blame you in any way. You did have hard times. You were woman enough to bear them. You won't have to bear them anymore. I know you are happy with God.

Mama, please forgive me for not writing to you, earlier. I didn't know your address. Please forgive me!

(Written a few days later):

Mama, I still can't believe you've left us to live with God. I hope you are happy. I wish you could have seen my ring, because you have always been so interested. I wish Paul could have met you. I know he would have loved you and I know you would have loved him, because our lives have been almost alike. Mama, I know it wasn't your fault you couldn't give us everything you wanted to. I hope you understand why we couldn't give you a Christmas gift. I really wanted to give you one but I didn't have any money. Oh, how I wish I could have given you some of the things I really wanted to.

I really won't forget you as long as I live. I can't believe you are dead and to keep you closer to my heart, I am going to pretend you are still living. In order to not think hard about you, now. . . I know it will hurt me if I do. I will close with this one question: You won't care if I take Paul's mother and pretend she is mine (you)? She is really so sweet and pretty, just as you were (and still are).

Bye, Bye, Mama. . . I hope to see you someday in heaven. . .

Lovingly Yours Always,
Your baby daughter, Jerrie

Before mama had passed away, I had moved from the WC Building to the Huffman Cottage. The girls from the Huffman Cottage and my housemother sent flowers to the Mills Home church in memory of her. This article was in the "Charity and Children" newspaper, which read: *"The beautiful flowers that graced the front of the Mills Home Church last Sunday were placed there by the Huffman Building girls in memory of Mrs. Hazel Payne, mother of Herman and Jerrie Canady. Jerrie Canady lives at Huffman and her cottage mates paid their respects through this medium."*

I had to begin thinking about what I wanted to do after graduation. I began to think that I wanted to be an airline stewardess for Eastern Airlines, stationed out of Miami, Florida. Anything I decided to do, I wanted to achieve in it. I began writing Eastern Airlines to acquire information on what steps I needed to take for acquiring a position with them.

(Huffman Cottage)

(Our group of girls at the Huffman Cottage)

(My senior photo)

(1961 senior class trip to Washington DC
[me first row, first left])

(Graduation class at Mills Home-1961
[me third from left, first row])

Our graduation was saddened by our little mascot, Stephanie, being killed in an auto accident, a few days prior to it. She was one of the prettiest little girls I had ever seen! She will always be remembered, especially by our Mills Home, 1961 graduation class.

(Stephanie Corder)

June, 1961, Paul and I graduated from high school and left Mills Home to live on our own.

My graduation, in 1961, left Herman as the only member of our family remaining at Mills Home.

The following was taken from the caseworker's records regarding Herman: *"Herman is a quiet boy and has a few close friends. He does not associate with a good number of the boys. He is electrically inclined and enjoys recreation quite a bit."*

I tried to be a big sister to my little brother and would try to visit with him as often, as possible. Once, he told me a boy in his cottage said to him, "Your mama is a whore!" (That is what the kids would say to other kids at the orphanage to upset them.) When he told me who had said it, I caught up with the boy in the Valley one night. I walked up to him and said, "Why did you say those bad things about my mama to my little brother?" He just stood there and looked and me. I swung back my hand and slapped him so hard on his little chubby cheeks. I thought I would be in real trouble, but I suppose he never reported it, realizing that he deserved it.

(Herman played baseball at Mills Home)   *(Herman's senior photo)*   *(Herman's navy photo)*

(Graduation class, 1964
[first row 2nd from right])

Herman would tease me, saying, "If you stood sideways and stuck your tongue out, you would look like a zipper!" I suppose it could have been worse!

My little brothers and I would argue and fight sometimes and I would tease them. They would get angry with me for teasing them. I was once wrestling with Robert Lee, while I was on vacation with daddy and accidentally hit him in his private area. He was crying and in such pain; I felt terrible for hurting him.

I learned my lesson, though; when Herman had had enough of my teasing him, he punched me in the stomach and knocked the air out of me. It hurt so bad, I never teased either of them again. Since then, I've always tried to be their big and loving sister.

(Robert Lee and Herman as teenagers)

Another one of my girlfriends at the orphanage was dating the superintendent's son and he had a car! Paul and I would double date with them at times. They eventually were married and we remained friends with them, even after graduation.

It seems all the children from Mills Home are bonded together as siblings, staying in touch throughout the years and always looking forward to seeing each other at homecoming each year. We don't have the opportunity to see each other as often as we would like.

Attached is a photo of one of my dear Mills home sisters that I have stayed in touch with throughout the years.

(Me & Bennie - 1960)

(Me & Bennie - 2013)

CHAPTER 16

AFTER GRADUATION, PAUL and I moved to Greensboro, North Carolina. I rented an upstairs apartment in a lady's home with another girl. Paul rented a room in another apartment house down the street, within walking distance to mine. We didn't have a car, so we had to walk everywhere we would go. He would walk over to my place and we would sit on the front porch to be together.

My first job out of high school was as a "Policy Writer" at Jefferson Standard Life Insurance Co., located on the seventeenth floor of the Jefferson Building, located in Greensboro, North Carolina. I had to walk to work throughout the summer, until we could afford a car.

This would turn out to be one of the worst jobs one could have. I filled out insurance forms eight hours a day, forty hours a week! My supervisor was an elderly lady who didn't like any of the younger employees. She seemed to dislike "youth" in our office! She was always standing over our shoulders and watching what we were typing, and criticizing us in any way she could. She would upset me so bad at times that I would go into the bathroom window and look down, seventeen stories, wondering how it might feel to jump. However, after pondering about it, I would come to my senses!

I worked there for about one year, and after leaving the company I heard she had lost her mind and had gone berserk. One day she was spotted running down the street, naked! So sad, but she made a lot of employees very miserable. I suppose karma finally caught up with her.

Paul got a job with JP Stevens, in Greensboro, using the experience he had learned from the Print Shop at Mills Home. He was still waiting and hoping to hear back from the baseball scouts, however.

The summer months were busy with our new jobs and planning our upcoming wedding. The closer the date came, the more I was beginning to have second thoughts about our marriage. I told Paul that I felt we should begin seeing others; I wasn't sure about marriage, and maybe we should postpone our plans. He got upset and said that he loved me enough to make it work. When I saw his tears, I didn't want to hurt him and I didn't want to have to tell everyone that we were canceling our wedding plans so we continued with the plans.

We had discussions with the pastor at Mills Home, Mr. Roger Williams, who was planning to marry us. It seemed to us that he was trying to talk us out of marriage and convince us that maybe we were too young. However, we continued on with our plans.

Neither of us had ever had a normal family life and we felt this was a good time to make a normal family life, together.

We needed to find a home and buy an automobile before our wedding. Our first automobile was a 1959 Ford Edsel. It was a blue and white convertible with white leather interior and was all automatic. I wish we still owned that Edsel; it would be a collectible today.

We found a home to rent that had five rooms, a bath, and of course, one of the rooms was turned into a pack room, just as I had always been accustomed to.

(Mills Home Baptist Church)

(Rev. Roger Williams)

We were married on August 29, 1961 in the Mills Home Baptist Church, by, Rev. Roger E. Williams. Mr. & Mrs. Quinn were wonderful in helping us plan the wedding. Mrs. Quinn helped me get my wedding gown, flowers, and the plans together. She also, made the beautiful wedding cake and held the reception at her home following the wedding. They are a lovely couple.

(Mr. and Mrs. Quinn, my caseworker at Mills Home - 2013)

[In memory of Mr. Afton Quinn: November 24, 1930 – June 19, 2015 "From the mystery of God we come – to the mystery of God we go. And the coming and going and everything in between, a gracious gift."]

In attendance at our wedding were all the children from Mills Home, my dear family from Durham, some of the workers from the orphanage, daddy and Martha, Robert Lee, and Herman. Jo was my matron of honor and my maids of honor were Dixie and Theresa (my close friends from Mills Home). Alice Faye and Pat were unable to attend this special occasion with us.

(Daddy walking me Down the Aisle)

We went on our honeymoon to Charlotte, North Carolina. The following weekend we went to the NASCAR races at Darlington, South Carolina, with our dear friends, Dixie and Mickey.

We rented our first home, a furnished home on Lowdermilk Street, in Greensboro, North Carolina. "Crash Craddock," a singer just becoming popular, lived across the street from us. He sounded like Elvis Presley, and he was pretty well known around Greensboro. It seemed he would go out and wash his car in "Speedos" when I would be out gardening in our yard. One day, I couldn't handle it any longer, and yelled across the street at him, "You think you are hot stuff, but, I can tell you, you're not!" He just looked at me and continued working. (I suppose I had to yell that remark to someone during my lifetime, since it was yelled at me, once?) He was most likely thinking, who is that crazy woman over there?

When Paul and I first got married, I had an uncontrollable temper and I now realize that he had the right temperament to be able to handle me. He was low key and hardly ever showed his anger. As I got older and more mature, I learned more and more to control the anger I had kept bottled inside me for all those years.

Once, Alice was visiting us from California with her three children. After staying with us for quite a while, I suppose Paul's patience was growing thin. One night when we came back from the grocery store the kids were in the back seat jumping around and yelling at each other and Paul reached back and smacked one of them on the head and said, "Shut Up!"

Alice turned to him and said, "Did you hit one of my kids?" Paul became so upset that he pulled into the driveway, got out of the car, grabbed a bag of groceries, dropped it and kicked the bag all the way across the front yard! (I found a can of grape juice in the front ditch, days later.) Alice and I still laugh when we talk about it, now.

Paul and I wanted so bad to have a baby. We tried for three years, but nothing seemed to work and I was getting more and more depressed. When the ladies at work would become pregnant, I would be so jealous. We were beginning to think I would never be able to have a child. I was wondering if maybe it was because I'd had an umbilical hernia when I was a baby.

We did not stay long in this home because we had an opportunity to take a travelling job with a department store chain, as auditors. We sold our 1959 Edsel and purchased a more fuel-efficient car, a Mercury Comet. Since we were in a furnished house, we didn't have furniture to get rid of so we went on the road. We were travelling with another girl from Mills Home, Barbara, along with her husband, James, who had been reared at Kennedy Home in Pembrook, North Carolina.

It was fun to be able to travel all over the Southeast and be able to stay in motels. But, it was a job and we had work to do in the evenings, calculating and writing up reports. We never had a lot of time for sightseeing or fun things.

Our job description was called "checkers." We would check the cashiers at different Department Stores. We would purchase an item, giving the cashier a large bill, causing them to need to give us change back; then, we would buy a second item, giving them the exact amount of "cash." This would allow them not to have to open the cash register. It was surprising to us, and the managers, how many cashiers would just pocket the "cash" that was given to them. We had to do a little acting so as not to blow our cover. Acting was right up my alley!

While in Texas, I became ill, vomiting, and it seemed to get worse as we traveled. I lay in the back seat while Paul drove. He would say that he felt like he was driving an ambulance. It was in the middle of summertime in the South and I was miserable!

I began craving green apples and green peaches, so we would stop by the roadside fruit stands to get them. My sickness got worse; we began thinking that I may be pregnant. We decided to go back home so I could get to a doctor for a checkup. I was very pregnant with our first baby! We were so elated!

We had a hard time finding a place to live and ended up renting a little trailer, in Thomasville, until we could find a home. It was so tiny, but it was a roof over our heads. This was during President Kennedy's assassination by Lee Harvey Oswald. I heard it on television that morning as I was getting out of the shower. By this time I was four months pregnant with my first child.

Before the baby was born, we found a little, two-room house, with one bath, on Haywood Street. The living area and bedroom area was combined. We cleaned it up and painted it and it was kind of cute. It was located close by our friends' (Dixie and Mickey) home. Now, we could spend a lot of time with them at dinner, etc.

A sweet little boy, Richard Jerome, was born in March, 1964. He was almost ten pounds (nine pounds, fifteen and a half ounces)! He was a darling, blue-eyed baby boy. He was the love of our lives!

(Richard Jerome)

We called him Ricky, and I always told him never to let anyone begin calling him "Dick"; that could be a nickname for Richard. He was an "all boy," so to speak, from the day he was born.

He was bottle fed, so that allowed me to go back to work when he was only six weeks old. In 1960s, companies weren't as understanding with new mothers and fathers, allowing them to take off work longer with a newborn, as they are today.

Paul and his friend, Freddie, began a plastics company in the basement of the Midway Drive-In, a hamburger restaurant in Thomasville. He worked long hours and late up into the night. Lots of time and energy went into starting the business. They needed more money to really get the business going, so soon others came into the company with money to help support it. They named the company Southern Film Extruders. Freddie and Paul were never general managers, but they worked in high positions in the company. Freddie passed away but Paul still worked there until his retirement.

Paul and I would go visit his mother, Isabelle, in Charlotte, where she managed a homecare for the elderly. Sometimes, however, the women she cared for were a scary to me. I would be afraid to sleep there because they would scream out loud at times, cussing and raving. After living with my daddy, yelling, cussing and raving around our house as a child, it upsets me to hear anyone raise his or her voice.

Isabelle would let us sleep in her bed to help me feel safe. She had a lot of patience with those elderly ladies and was very good to them. It takes a special person to be able to care for the elderly. I don't think I could do it because they would remind me of the orphanage matrons!

Our close friends, Dixie and Mickey, never had children and they loved Ricky and enjoyed babysitting him. Ricky would get up on the couch and holler, "Bat Man!" Then, he would fall on the floor on his tummy. I would be so afraid that he would hurt himself. But they would laugh at him and that would cause him to do it more.

We remained at the two-room home on Haywood Street for about seven months before moving into a brick home on Clay Street where another one of our friends had lived and told us they were moving, so we called to check it out. It was larger than the house we were in, a three-room apartment with a living room, kitchen, bedroom, and a bathroom located off the screened-in back porch. This was a chilly, duplex apartment. It had two oil heaters, one in the living room and one in the bedroom. The bathroom on the screened in porch did not have any heat; we had to use an electric heater in it.

We didn't stay in this apartment very long before we were looking for a larger place to live. We found a duplex on Harris Street. It had two bedrooms, one bathroom, and a living room and kitchen combination. It was located closer to town and closer to the hospital and the baby's doctor.

We met nice friends across the street: Anita and Doug and their family of three boys. This gave Ricky friends to play with, and boy, did they play! Four boys were over at our house or over at their house all the time. Anita was an anesthesiologist at Thomasville Hospital, and once, when her son hit Ricky in the head with a hoe during their play, I had to call her over to take care of him. I couldn't handle seeing all the blood coming from Ricky's head. I was freaking out!

(Harris Street duplex)

I was employed at a Chinchilla Ranch in High Point, North Carolina. One of the managers knew my Uncle Gene and Aunt Nellie from Clayton, North Carolina. He said his daughter babysat their children when they lived in Clayton. He was nice to work with and we got along fine. However, he didn't get along with the owner of the company. Each of them would become upset with one another and yell and then one would slam the door and leave. Eventually, the owner sold the company to him. I worked there until I became pregnant with my second child.

When I awoke to sickness again, I knew the feeling; I was pregnant. A beautiful baby girl was born in November, 1966. Her name was Paula Michelle, weighing in at seven pounds, seven ounces. She was a beautiful baby! We were so proud of her. Ricky was now a big brother at two and a half years old.

(Paula Michelle)

During the time of my pregnancy with Paula, I felt I must have "marked" her because of her love for animals! Paul had gotten me a darling little puppy (beagle), like I had always wanted. One day I let it out in the front yard to run around and play. While I was out there with it, our neighbor drove up into their driveway and the puppy went running over to her car and she ran over it. I was devastated and crying and screaming for her to stop before it was too late! I became very emotional, which is common during pregnancy.

In a couple of days, we returned home to find a dog tied to our clothes line! Paul went over to talk to our neighbor and she said she had gotten us another dog. No way did I want another dog at this time (especially an old, fat, dog). I was not one bit appreciative. To make things worse, when I tried to feed it, it growled at me! I would not keep a dog that would bite the hand that fed it. I asked Paul to tell her to get rid of it! He told me that she was only trying to help! But, I refused to see it that way. The dog was gone the very next day.

The Easter after Paula was born, we got Ricky and Paula two baby ducks. They were so cute and they would follow us around the yard and we would have a great time playing with them—until one day when I arrived home from work and they had stripped all my tomato plants! It was time to take them to the pond (in the Holly Hill cemetery); that's where people took ducks when they didn't want them any longer (after Easter). We would go there to visit them, often.

(Me, Ricky, and Paula)

(Paul, Ricky, and Paula)

Herman came to live with us prior to joining the navy after graduation. He had so much fun playing around with Ricky and he loved him so much. Herman was always trying to make him tougher. He and Robert Lee, both, were very good uncles to our children.

(Robert Lee, Herman, and Paul, Ricky and Paula)

Herman was stationed in Norfolk, Virginia, after receiving his training in San Diego, California. Then, he was on the aircraft carrier, the "Enterprise," in the Mediterranean. When he returned from duty overseas he came to visit us and he would bring his navy buddy, Ken, with him. Paul and I thought a lot of Ken and treated him like family.

One night he wanted Paul and I to drive him back out to the interstate highway, so, he could hitchhike back to the Naval Base in Norfolk, Virginia. It was pouring down rain and I wanted to take him all the way back to Norfolk. We took him quite a ways and then had to drop him off. I cried all the way back home. It was so sad to see him standing out there in the rain waiting for a ride and not knowing how long he would be standing there.

I would send him brownies, photos, etc. while he was overseas. Paul felt as if he was a brother to all my brothers and sisters and they felt the same way, because we were all reared at Mills Home, together. To this day, my brothers and sisters feel like he is family.

I acquired a position as sales secretary to the sales manager at a TV station, in High Point, North Carolina. I loved my job and it was exciting.

(Me, at the TV station)

The New York Broadcasting group would come to High Point, North Carolina, having large events at The Top of the Mart Furniture Expo Building. Some of the women from the television station would be hostess for the events. I always enjoyed the glitter and glamour of the events.

I would fill in for the show "Dialing for Dollars," a popular television show in the 1960s. I was beginning to get noticed by the public as a television personality and it felt good to me.

While working in the sales department and spending time on television, I was asked how I would like to be a "Romper Room" teacher, having to go to New York for training? I was really debating whether or not to try it. However, I had two babies at home and Paul would not like me being away from home.

The station allowed Ricky to be on "Romper Room" when he was only four. A child needed to be in kindergarten before they were allowed to be on the show. But, because I was working there, they allowed it. I remember him not paying any attention to the teacher and just walking around looking at the lights.

Paul saw a change in me and I knew I was changing, too. I was becoming very unhappy with our married life and getting more and more bored with it. I was feeling as if I was missing out on life; that

I was only good for working, having babies, and keeping house. I needed more of an exciting life!

I asked Paul many times to please move from Thomasville because being reared there at the orphanage, I felt that I needed to see more of the world and go places. However, Paul was happy just staying put.

He felt that my job was the problem and he always wanted me to quit. I told him I would get away for a while to think about things and see if I could come to terms with my feelings.

In the summer of 1969 (during the first landing on the moon), I flew to California to visit my sister, Alice, and her husband, Leonard and their family. I spent a couple of weeks with them.

While talking to Alice about my feelings, she told me I would come to terms with my emotions and she felt I would make a wise decision. What came out of our discussions, however, was that I had always felt like Paul was a brother to me, rather than a lover or a husband. He was a wonderful man and a good father and I felt so guilty putting him through the ups and downs of my emotions. He was always trying to appease me and do whatever it took to make me happy.

Coming back from my visit, I still had the same feelings of not wanting to be married. So, I approached Paul saying that we needed to separate. He became really upset and asked me to get in the car and go for a ride to talk about it. Since my brother, Herman, was there visiting from the navy he wanted to be alone.

He drove up a country back road and began speeding up. I asked him to slow down and he just kept stepping on the gas and then floored it. It scared me so bad, I yelled at him, "Go ahead—go ahead and kill me and get me out of my misery!" Somehow, my words shocked him and he slowed down; we began to talk in a normal tone. Soon, Paul said that he would get a place to live outside of our home to allow me the space and time to find myself.

He got an apartment in High Point, which was closer to his work. The children would go visit him and I would go with them at times.

Paul was still feeling like it was my job at the TV station that was making me act so "crazy."

After a few months, we decided to get back together and give our marriage a second chance. We did move away from Thomasville. We moved to Enterprise Street, in Greensboro, North Carolina.

It was a cute home with a fenced-in backyard, perfect for Ricky and Paula. They had friends who lived across the street from our house. This home backed up to a greenbelt. It had three bedrooms, a living room, a kitchen, a bath, and a garage. I had a nice yard for my gardening.

(Paula and Ricky)

I continued to work at the television station and our marriage was doing okay. But, I was still wondering, "Is this all there is in life?" Paul still insisting that the television station was the reason for my unhappiness, I felt I had no other choice but to prove to him by quitting my job. I didn't work the rest of the summer.

I had begun taking the birth control pills after Paula was born, because we felt we had our family; a boy and a girl. However, when we split up for a few months, I had gotten off the pill. After we had gotten back together, the pill had not taken effect and I discovered that I was pregnant again! This was in December, 1969. Ricky was five years old and Paula was three years old.

One day during my pregnancy, Ricky, Paula and I were out in the back yard and an airliner flew over the woods behind our house and looked as if it was going to crash. We lived in the path of the airlines from the Greensboro airport. I quickly grabbed the children and ran inside, thinking it was going to crash into our backyard! We just sat and waited for the big crash. I looked out the window just in time to see it lift up and began climbing higher and higher out of site. We never heard anything on the news about it.

We bought a new Ford Station Wagon, large enough for our family. We were also in the planning stages of building our home in Trinidad, a suburb of High Point, North Carolina. Building a home was a stressful situation, especially with me being pregnant. I was out there almost every day trying to get things completed and getting subcontractors on the job. They kept promising that it would be done by the time the baby came. I had a temper, and showed it at times to the subs. Our contractor lived a few houses down the street, so he could watch the job better than most contractors and we trusted him to get it completed on time. There were still items that had not been completed prior to our moving in.

(Our First Home in the Trinidad [now])

While I was in the hospital having my third baby, Robert Lee had gotten out of the navy and was able to come over to help Paul move us into our new home. It was a split-level home and seemed perfect for our family. It would be nice to get out of the hospital and go right into our new home.

Our baby girl, Pamela Denise, was born in August, 1970. She was born in the High Point Hospital, while Ricky and Paula had been born in the Thomasville Hospital. She was so precious with her big brown eyes and dark hair.

(Pamela Denise)

Paul worked hard clearing the yard, while I was busy decorating the interior. Ricky's room was blue and white with double twin beds, and Paula's room was red and white, with a white canopy bed and white wicker dresser. We put the baby's crib in Paula's room.

There was straw thrown all over the lawn, covering the grass seed to germinate. Being located in a wooded area, there were a lot of snakes around our house. Once, while looking out the upstairs window, I could see a copperhead snake wiggling in the yard (the same color as the straw). Our kids were not allowed to go outside until the grass grew out.

Paul picked up a baby copperhead once, and stuck a stick down its throat, playing with it on our doorstep. I was upset with him because I didn't want the kids to think they could play with snakes!

We lived close to a small airport and while we were eating dinner at the table, we looked out the window, and low and behold, there was a parachute draped over our tree with a gentleman hanging on it! Paul went out to help him cut himself lose and get his parachute away from the branches. Ricky and Paula thought it was funny. . . we did, too!

I enjoyed planting azaleas, shrubbery, etc. in our beautiful tree-filled yard. Paul built a log fence around the front and it was looking nice after the clearing and planting. We always talked about building a carport and adding other features to our new home.

Being that we lived out in the country, we could shoot our gun. While we were sitting on the kitchen steps once, Paul handed his rifle to me and asked if I could shoot a jar that he had placed up the embankment. I shot at it and smashed the jar all to pieces! It surprised me and I'm sure it surprised him. Because of daddy's many rampages with his gun, I had always been afraid of them. But, I trusted Paul with his gun, and this was the first time I had ever shot one!

CHAPTER 17

WE NEEDED THE money so we decided that I should go back to work. I found a job at a New York Stock Exchange office in High Point. It was an interesting job, in that I ran the teletype line, making exchanges between High Point and New York. My fast typing skills paid off, because I had only seconds to relay from the brokers to the New York Stock Exchange. I would also give reports on the radio on the stock market status.

One of the stockbrokers became friends with me. He asked if he and his wife and Paul and I could get together sometime to play cards. After talking with Paul, we realized that we didn't have that many friends and thought it would be nice to get together. We began playing cards and going out to eat, etc., with our new friends.

They had a Mustang convertible, and we would go riding, the four of us together. His wife was a beautiful, tall, blonde lady; she could have been a model.

Things went well for a while. We had fun together. Once, while I was sitting in the back seat with his wife and he and Paul were in the front seat, he looked in his rear view mirror and winked at me. I had never thought of anything else between us until this incident. Then, while we were playing cards, he nudged my leg with his foot under the table. It embarrassed me, but I never mentioned it. I tried to stop things by not asking them over again to play cards.

At work, he continued wanting us to get together and flirting with me. It was flattering because I had never had anyone flirt with me like this. I just tried to do my job and ignore him, however. He would tell me how unhappy he was at home and how he was thinking of getting a divorce from his wife (the typical tales that men tell women). I continued trying to ignore him and concentrate on my job.

His wife and I had grown close and she would call me up, asking me to come over to talk to her about things going on in their marriage. While she would talk with me, I would feel like a hypocrite, knowing he was making advances at me at work. I would just say to her that they needed to talk and work it out among themselves. She would say that he wouldn't talk to her about anything!

Things in our house weren't the greatest at this time either. Paul was working long hours and I was home alone many, many nights with the children. I was trying to maintain a job, the home, and the children, and realized I was going back into the state of mind I had been in previously.

I told Paul how I was feeling and that I felt things weren't right between us, that we were just prolonging our marriage in trying to make it work. He became upset and kept trying to convince me I was wrong, until I finally had to go off, saying mean things to him, like, "I just don't love you!" I know it hurt him, but he wasn't listening to my feelings. I did love him, but not in the way as I should have or in the way he wanted me to love him. I told him, "I've given you the best years of my life and it's not fair to you by my staying in this marriage, feeling this way." He left and found an apartment in High Point and we were separated, again.

The broker separated from his wife, and soon thereafter he and I began a relationship. He was a prominent stockbroker; he was tall, good looking, and seemed to have a lot on the ball.

His wife worked for an attorney in High Point and she would call and talk with Paul. He told me she was so upset that she was going to file a "Breach of Promise" against me. If we had not known each other prior to our separation, it wouldn't have been so ugly. Paul was jealous of the broker and his wife was jealous of me. It got pretty ugly between us all.

The children told me later that Paul had come around our house one night with a gun while the broker was visiting me at our house. The neighbors even told me that they had also seen him driving around with a gun in the back seat. When I heard this, I decided I was leaving the house and finding another place to live!

I quit my job at the stockbroker's business but we continued seeing each other. I found a position at the health department in High Point. I enjoyed working with the nurses as a medical transcriber.

The stockbroker began staying at my house with me, until the tension began building up more and more between us. We took a trip to the beach and that's when I learned that he was a pool shark and a hustler. We would stop at pool halls on the way to the beach and he would hustle for money to pay for our trip. I would sit in the car and wait for him until he felt he had won enough money. This made me feel cheap. During this time, Paul said he had put a monitor on the car to determine where I had gone.

He began drinking heavily, drinking gin right out of the bottle and he would become so obnoxious. He would say over and over again that the kids were too much for him and he couldn't handle it. Then he would say things like, "I could find someone else if I wanted to." I became so tired of his actions and his remarks that one day, when he said, "I know where I can find someone else, if I wanted to," I said, "Go ahead; Go find someone If you want to." That very night he didn't come by after work and I never heard a word from him again.

After a few days, a girlfriend and I went driving around High Point and we saw his car in front of a girl's house; it was a girl who worked at the local bank. I knew, then, that he had been unfaithful to me. So I called and left a message on his phone, saying that by the time I got off of work I wanted his things—all of them—out of my house! The next day when I got home after work, his things were gone. I have always been too proud to follow and chase after anyone. I wasn't about to begin doing it then!

I went for days thinking I would die from heartache. My left arm ached and I actually thought I was having a heart attack. Paul came by and stayed with me and tried to console me. It did help having him there and having someone to talk to. I don't know if I could have made it without him. Paul was so attentive and understanding and never tried to talk about our relationship at all during that time. It was truly wonderful to have him care that much for me. I realized he loved me, unconditionally.

I had thought many times of going back to him, but just didn't trust my being able to stay with him. I've always told the children that he is a good father and a wonderful person, but I just always felt like he was more of a brother to me.

This had been the first time in my life I honestly thought I was in love with someone, and for this to happen, for him to deceive me this way, was unbearable. I learned the feeling of "heartbreak," for sure.

I went to the doctor's office and was told I had arthritis in my left arm and that was what was causing the pain. I had to wear a sling on my arm for a couple of weeks. It did interfere with my job; however, I managed to get by.

Our home in Trinidad went into foreclosure because I couldn't make the payments alone. We lost the car and our home. When there is a divorce you lose most everything, and sometimes even the friends you had acquired.

In the meantime, I found a house on the north side of High Point. It was very small, but because I could get away from our home and the familiarity of everything, it was a safe haven, and the stockbroker would not know where I had moved.

Paul would visit and we would have dinner together, and yes, he would stay overnight at times. But, this didn't last long. The children loved for him to be there. I felt I was doing the right thing by allowing it for the kids, but he was expecting us to go back into our marriage. I knew I could not put him through the heartache again. So, I told him he couldn't stay with us any longer and it was best for all of us. The kids had hopes, too, that we would get back together.

Eventually, I found a townhouse on the south side of High Point. It was in an urban development townhouse and the price was right and it was newly built and close to shopping. The builder and I worked out a deal, and I purchased it. If I ever decided to leave the townhouse, it would automatically go back to him.

I enjoyed my job at the health department and met some really nice friends. One of the ladies and I became very close friends. She was very religious and I admired her. Her husband was a heavy drinker and she had two precious children. Her husband rebuilt a

Volkswagon Bug for me. They were wonderful friends.

Once, my girlfriend, Anita, and I went to the beach together. Her mother lived close to Myrtle Beach, so we stayed with her while we were there.

One evening, while we were out, we met a group of people and there was one guy who stood out in the crowd. He wasn't dressed in uniform, but I found out that he was in the navy. Since I had two brothers in the navy, we had lots to talk about. He lived in Southern California and was stationed on the East Coast. I was infatuated with him and found out he had been divorced for two years. Anita thought he was a catch, and I valued her opinion. After talking with him for awhile, I felt as if I had known him for a long time.

We talked a lot on the phone and he began driving up to visit me on the weekends, when he was off duty. The children liked him and he was good with them.

When his naval duties were completed, he planned to head back to California and drive his car across country. It was hard to say good-bye, but he said if I ever got out that way to call him. I didn't want to see him go but I always thought I would be out in California, anyway, someday.

As time went by, Paul began trying to talk me into us getting back together, and each time he would bring it up, I would become upset. He would come over to get the children for a visit and would be teary-eyed and would want me to go with them wherever they went somewhere. I refused because I didn't want to give him false hopes. He would come by late at night and sometimes in the early mornings, checking up on what I was doing. It became unbearable for me, and even though I had just moved into my new townhouse, I made another decision to leave, altogether. My townhouse would go back to the builder!

I had always thought about moving to California. My sister now lived in Northern California, my sailor friend, lived in Southern California. Looking at the map, they look fairly close together. I remember thinking I could stay at my sister's house in Northern California and work in San Francisco (200 miles away). Boy, that was a wild thought!

The more I thought about it, the more I liked the idea. I would just get the heck away from High Point and Thomasville. I would get away from the memories of the orphanage, Paul, the stockbroker and everything around High Point and Thomasville. It was time to start a new life!

I called my sister, Jo, who lived in Alexandria, Virginia, and told her I wanted to leave the area and go to California to be near Alice. She said she would come and pick me up and take me back to her home and I could fly out of Dullas Airport, which was close to where she lived.

It was 1971; I had sold or had given away all of the furniture, toys, and clothes that we could not take with us and I gave my VW Bug back to my friend's husband who had built it for me. I would use the money that I got off our belongings to start over again. Jo drove from Virginia to pick me and my three children up, along with what little belongings we could carry.

Paul came over to tell the children good-bye prior to our leaving and left a note for us on the kitchen counter on a piece of blue paper, which read, *"Ricky, Paula, and Pam, I will always love you and will miss you . . . you, too, Goldie! Love you, Dad."* I have kept that piece of blue paper in my possession all these years, along with the love letters he wrote during our dating time. (I kept them for the children when they grew up.)

We stayed in Alexandria for about a week prior to flying out to Redding, California, where we would begin a new life. It was a sad day when we left for the airport. Jo and I cried and I was so frightened thinking what life would be like in a strange state and town. It was sad to be leaving her and all my memories in North Carolina, knowing that I would never be back there to live.

CHAPTER 18

UPON ARRIVING IN Redding, I got off the airplane and looked up and the sky was as blue as I had ever seen it before. My brother-in-law had come to pick us up in a big green Cadillac, with no air condition! The weather was dry and very hot. The temperature was 113 degrees! I had never experienced it so hot! I almost began to cry, thinking I had made a wrong decision and this was feeling like hell on earth!

It seemed we had driven for many miles before coming to their double-wide manufactured home up in the hills close to Shingletown, California. We were surrounded with red clay and lava rock and there was no green vegetation anywhere, only dry, dusty manzanita bushes.

When we arrived at their home, Alice was sitting on the front steps with all the doors and windows in the house wide open. I don't think even an air conditioner could have handled the extreme heat on that particular day! Thank goodness it would be cooling off in the evening.

Their home was located between Redding and Shingletown, in the foothills of Mount Lassen, and the property had lava rock from centuries ago that had been thrown on their property by the devastating eruption of Mount Lassen in 1915 (see below).

"On May 22, 1915, an explosion at Lassen Peak, California (also known as Mt. Lassen), the southernmost active volcano in the Cascade Range, devastated nearby areas and rained volcanic ash as far away as 200 miles to the East. This explosion was the most powerful in a 1914-1917 series of eruptions that were the last to occur in the Cascades before the 1980 eruption of Mt. St. Helens, in Washington State."

(May, 1915 Mt. Lassen eruption)

(Today)

The red clay in their yard would stick to my feet when I would go barefoot. I helped Leonard work in the yard and tried to get it cleared of lava rock, weeds, etc. It took forever to get my feet clean and the red dirt out of my toenails. I really missed the green vegetation that I had always been familiar with!

Leonard was an excellent musician and Alice and I enjoyed watching him play in his gigs all around Redding, and going out to dinner and dancing. They had lived there for many years and knew a lot of people and I got to meet many of their friends.

(Leonard and Alice Faye)   *(Leonard with his "Top Hat" Group)*

It was wonderful to see my sister and her family again, and had fun visiting with them, but knew I didn't wish to stay there to live. So, I had to make up my mind as to where I wanted to live and what to do as far as work, before the little money I had was gone.

I had my sights set on Southern California, since that was where they had lived previously, when I had visited them earlier in 1969. I had really liked the Southern California atmosphere; it was exciting to me.

Away, Away, Away down South, in Dixie...

CHAPTER 19

ALICE AGREED TO keep the children while I travelled down to Southern California to see if that would be a better place for us to live. She was unhappy that I was going, but I knew that my sailor friend whom I had met in North Carolina lived there and just maybe he and I could reconnect.

I boarded a Greyhound bus to Southern California and called him to say I was coming down; he invited me to come and stay with him, his sister and brother-in-law in Glendora, California until I found my own place.

We reconnected, and began dating. We took several trips to see his parents in Victorville, California. I met his sisters and their family. My being a country girl, it was nice knowing a family in such a large and scary area. He had a very nice family and I enjoyed spending time with them.

I soon found a two-bedroom, one-bath apartment in West Covina. It was an upstairs unit. It was unfurnished and remained that way for a long time. I had to sleep on the carpet floor until I found a double bed that someone in the apartment unit was selling.

After purchasing the bed, I decided I needed a car. I saw in the newspaper that someone was selling their car; a small, green, foreign car (not even knowing the make/model). My friend took me to pick it up and I was so happy to finally have wheels, again! This little car took me to a lot of places around Los Angeles. I was so intimidated by the freeways; they seemed too busy and scary to me, and I would take the side roads to avoid the freeway traffic.

Once, while I was driving down to Victorville to visit my sailor's family, I had to get onto the freeways. I got confused and didn't know where I was and couldn't decide what direction I was headed. I knew I had to make a decision, so I pulled on to the off-ramp. I ended up in the middle of the median. It wasn't five seconds before a highway patrolman pulled up and asked me what I was doing sitting there. I told him I was new to the area and didn't know where I was going. He saw that I was shaken up and told me to go ahead on up the ramp; it was the correct direction to Victorville.

While driving over the Cucamonga pass, since I wasn't accustomed to driving in the mountains, I didn't realize I had to change gears going straight up the mountain. I kept it in third gear all the way up and I was just creeping and letting other cars fly by me; they would pass me hollering, "Come on, come on!" They were motioning like they were trying to help me up the mountain. I was so humiliated after realizing what I was doing wrong!

In West Covina, I found a position as a typist at a company that was family owned. It was located just a few blocks from my apartment. I was the only employee who wasn't a member of their family. They were so rude to me and I never felt wanted or appreciated. After a couple of weeks, it became so unbearable that one day I went home for lunch and I never returned to work. When they called me, I told them they were rude and that no one would work in a place feeling the way they had made me feel. It was the second worst job I had ever worked!

I wondered what I was going to do now that I had quit my job. I continued looking for work, even though I was having second thoughts about remaining in the area. I knew I didn't want to go back up to Shingletown to live. So I continued looking for work.

I felt lucky that I found a job at a company in Azusa, California and that would allow me to drive to work by using the side roads and not the freeways. My position was secretary in the purchasing department. I met friends there and felt like I was finally finding my place and was on my way to a new life in Southern California.

I wanted to have my children down in Southern California with me, so I looked in the paper and found two single beds and purchased them for the children. Beds were the only furnishings I had in the apartment.

I was really missing my children and wanted to go back to Northern California to get them and bring them down to West Covina. My sailor friend and I drove up to Shingletown and he was able to meet my sister and brother-in-law and we spent a few days with them. They seemed to like him a lot, too.

(Pam, Ricky, and Paula)

He drove me and the children back down to Southern California. Soon after we got back to West Covina, I realized they needed a TV. We found someone in Pasadena who was selling hers and I took the children to pick it up, still taking the side roads. We didn't have cable, but it was okay just getting a few pictures with the help of rabbit ears.

It was good having the children back with me and they had play-mates throughout the apartment units. The apartment was located close to shopping, but seemed more protected due to the layout. It was built in a square with a courtyard in the middle. It also had a pool and the school was close by; they would go play in the schoolyard. In those days, we didn't have to worry so much about kids being alone in public places. They would also walk a block to Jack in the Box, one of their favorite places to eat.

Ricky was eight years old and Paula was six and Pam was four. A lady in the downstairs apartment would babysit Pam and look after Ricky and Paula after school, until I arrived home from work each day.

My sailor and I became more and more estranged from each

other. Having three children was a big responsibility for a guy who had no children. He seemed to be too busy with his life and I needed company and felt so alone, even though I had my children with me. I would call my sister's friend in Shingletown to have Alice call me. When she called me I would tell her how alone I was feeling. She gave me a name of a friend they had known in the entertainment field. They thought I would like him or at least have someone to talk to. I called him and left a message, but never heard back. Being proud as I was, I never attempted to call him again.

I saw on the bulletin board in the complex that a lady downstairs wanted to sell her kitchen table and chairs for $20. Since we didn't have a table to eat on, I asked her if I could purchase it and give her the $20 when I got paid. She said it was okay and we finally had a kitchen table. (Didn't have much food, but we had a table.)

The money I had saved had disappeared when I purchased the car. I would make macaroni and tomatoes many times for us to eat. There were times that I would mash up vanilla wafers to feed the children. I was beginning to think I had made another bad decision by bringing the children down to Southern California. Many times, I wished I had never left North Carolina. But just when I would begin to give up, something would happen that made me think things would be okay.

There was a guy who worked at Merritt Products by the name of Bill who kept asking me out to dinner. There was just something about him that I didn't like, or my intuition was telling me not to get involved with him. I just couldn't put my finger on it, at the time.

I asked employees around the company about him and my girlfriend, Sue, told me to go ahead and go to dinner with him, that he seemed like an okay guy. She said that if I didn't like him I wouldn't have to go out with him again. So I finally decided to go to dinner, and we both had a relaxing and great time.

Bill was handsome and resembled William Holden. He had a beautiful smile and was very courteous. He had been divorced for a few years and had a daughter and a son. Both were teenagers. His son loved racing dirt bikes and was really good at it. We would take all the children to watch him in his races on the weekends when Bill had visiting privileges with his children.

He had his own apartment and that was nice because sometimes I wanted my own privacy. He would come over to my place and sometimes we would go over to his apartment.

He seemed like a very nice fellow and I enjoyed having an adult to talk to and go places with. We began seeing each other more and more.

He drove us back up to Shingletown to visit with Alice and her family. He liked them and they liked him. We went to Disneyland, car races, Havasu and Virginia City, Arizona. He had a boat and we would go skiing and boating on the Colorado River. Things seemed good for a short while and he would take me and the children to lots of places; Universal Studios, Catalina Island, Reno and Las Vegas.

(Bill liked for me to dress this way.)

Bill had never known his real dad and he had a younger sister. His mother was a religious woman. We would go to the Holiness church with her in Riverside, California. When the church people started jumping and screaming "in tongues" and the preacher came toward me to push me to fall to the floor like the others who were falling on the floor, I said, "Don't touch me!" He looked at me weird and backed off. It frightened me because it brought back all those memories of people screaming in the Holiness church when I was a little girl.

Bill told me horrible things his mother had said to him as a little boy. She would say things like, "You make me sick!" She once said to him (in front of me), "If you ever do anything to hurt her, I will disown you." He never felt like he measured up to what his mother wanted of him.

He had recently broken up with his girlfriend, but was still talking about her and trying to watch her in everything she did. I felt this was unusual and told him so. But, he would say that he and she had been together a long time and he was concerned about her. He was most likely still seeing her, but since I was so trustworthy at that time, I never really thought of it.

The more we were together the more I began to see things I didn't like in him. It seemed that he would be happy and outgoing one moment and the next moment he would be depressed.

He got really upset with Paul because he wasn't paying child support for the children and he was helping me out with food, etc. He demanded that I go down to the welfare department and sign up for welfare and turn Paul in for not helping out with the children.

Going down to the county welfare's office was one of the lowest points in my life. I never thought I would be at the welfare office begging for help. I just sat there, crying and telling them how bad things were at home, financially. They took down all the information on Paul and contacted him at his work, demanding child support.

It was all I could do with my salary to keep the lights turned on and have a phone and put food on the table. (Paul did send one check; however, it bounced.)

One day Bill went over to his ex-girlfriend's house. He was there for hours! His grandma called me to please go over to his ex-girlfriend's house. She and his grandpa were there and apparently there had been a fight. I got in the car, with the children, and immediately drove over. When I got there the police were there with their lights on and had the house surrounded and their guns pulled. It scared me so much that I just drove by and came back home because it was getting dark and I also had the children with me.

I lay there all night wondering what the heck was going on over there and wondering if he had been shot. The next morning, his grandma was on the phone crying and asking me to go over there, again. She couldn't even talk she was crying so hard. I really thought he had been shot.

I asked my neighbor to watch the children and got in my car and drove over. When I got into the house, Bill was like a crazy man, on the floor fighting with his ex-girlfriend with his grandma begging him to stop. I screamed at him to stop and he looked up at me with his eyes bewildered and said, "You go in there and call your sorry husband to send child support!" I went into the bathroom and called Paul and told him what was going on and he couldn't believe what was happening. He said he would send some support. I went back and told Bill that I had called Paul.

Eventually, Bill calmed down and apologized to everyone, saying he was upset because she was seeing someone else. I couldn't believe what I was hearing because he was seeing someone else too and why did it matter to him?

I left him there and went back home, thinking, "What have I gotten myself into?" I was wondering what I was going to do. I was so mad at him and kept saying to myself that if I had the money, I would leave here, now. He eventually came over, apologizing and saying how sorry he was about what he had done; he admitted he had been out of line. My feelings for him were quickly changing.

His grandma and grandpa and I became very close. I would take the children over to their home in Pasadena and spend a lot of time with them. They had moved to the west coast from Oklahoma and she taught me to read cards. I always loved playing cards, but, after learning to read them, it made a difference in my game. I knew what each card stood for and I would read hers and she would read mine. But, I began to think it was the devil at work, something I learned from my upbringing.

One day while we were driving through downtown his grandma got upset with me when I told her that I thought Bill was psychotic and needed counseling. I felt close enough to her to let her know my feelings about him. All of a sudden she jumped out of the car when it came to a stop, yelling at me and telling me I had no right to talk that way about him. She was in denial saying there was nothing wrong with him.

I insisted that she get back in the car. I didn't want to leave her standing there in the street, downtown. She got back in, and from that day forward I never felt the same about her, either.

Bill's mother came over, saying that Bill had a real problem. She told me that he had been that way most of his adult life! She also said that Bill loved me so much and if anyone could help him, I could! So in my mind, I felt good that I could help him.

The police filed a report regarding the incident with his ex-girlfriend and it was recommended that he be admitted to Norwalk Hospital for observation. He was there for a couple of weeks. His mother and I would go visit him and he would be so doped up he couldn't even talk straight. After a while, he was diagnosed with schizophrenia and was put on medication.

After his release from the hospital, he seemed to act even more unusual. He started suggesting that we have a threesome in sex. He asked me to ask my girlfriend and even my cousin who lived in Pasadena, if they would join us! He was becoming more and more involved in porno, wanting me to watch stag movies with him. The whole idea was irritating and disgusting to me. I would just listen to him and block out the things he would say. I was becoming even more distant with him with each day that passed.

I had talked with some of the ladies in the complex about him and they would laugh at the things he would say. They would say, "Let's all get together and f--- his brains out! He became a joke. It was getting embarrassing for me to hear them talk about it. I was still thinking that maybe I could help him.

In the meantime, my previous sailor friend got in touch with me and told me he wanted to see me again. So I went out with him a few times and tried to cool it with Bill. However, he told me he didn't understand the hold that Bill had on me. He said when he and I had dated, previously, that I was a strong person and had made my own decisions. He said it appeared that I had changed and I didn't seem to be the same person. We eventually parted ways for good. I suppose I had changed a bit.

When I think back, I realize that I was afraid of Bill and his behavior and tried not to set him off. I still thought that I could help him, even though it was like being around a time bomb. I believed his behavior came from the way he was treated as a young boy. He always felt his mother didn't love him, especially when she would say the mean things to him. I was beginning to feel sorry for him.

I was starting to think the children were not safe around him anymore. He was getting too strict with them. We took the boat to the Colorado River in Havasu, Arizona many times. He would try to make Paula get into the Colorado River to ski when she didn't want to, making her cry. At times he would try to help her with her homework, and when she didn't understand it he would scream at her and upset her until she cried. I would have to tell him to stop and leave her alone. I never knew when he would fly off the handle at them.

Bill was really hard on Rick, him being a boy. He expected him to be perfect and even used a belt on him once when he did something he was told not to do. He was so rough with him that I had to go in and make him stop spanking him. Pam was a baby, so he didn't have much to do with her. But he always seemed to be picking on Paula and Rick, and would do so until they cried. Bill didn't have a lot to do with his own kids, either, except going to watch his son at his bike races. I guess he treated children like his father treated him.

Bill began trying hard to act normal again, but I didn't trust him with his emotions. I called Paul and asked him if he would come out to California to get the children for a while for their safety, until I could get settled and figure out what I could do.

Paul flew out and picked up the children and took them back to North Carolina. At least I wouldn't have to worry about their safety anymore.

Paul was most likely thinking I would eventually go back to North Carolina too. It was sad to see them all leave. I began to think that Paul and I hadn't had such a bad life after all!

CHAPTER 20

I WAS SO stressed with Bill's behavior that it was affecting my work. One day at work, while I was on the phone with a debtor, my supervisor, a young son of one of the managers, told me to get off the phone. I was so upset that I just looked at him and said, "I quit!" So I got up and walked out. The manager called me to come back and I told her I was leaving the area, anyway, and I didn't appreciate a kid (wet behind his ears) telling me I couldn't be on the phone. I never went back.

I had been thinking of leaving Bill for a while. He had quit his job, too, and wanted us to move to Havasu, Arizona. I hadn't made up my mind about what I could do, so I went along with him. We packed up his truck with his furniture and what little I had and headed for Havasu.

We found a duplex, two-bedroom, one-bath, located on a hillside overlooking Havasu and the Colorado River. It duplex had a lot of cactus around the unit and I loved to work in the yard, even though it was 113 degrees in the shade. I could think about other things while I was gardening—pleasant thoughts.

It was so hot, but since Bill had his boat we would take advantage of the river whenever we could. We would just go cruising under the London Bridge and around the golf course and campground.

The sunsets were magnificent! I spent many nights driving down to the river, alone, just sitting there watching the sunsets.

We went to see a show down in the little village below the London Bridge. It was a Conway Tweedy concert and we got mooned by a spectator, running across the stage and then the bridge!

Living away from his ex-girlfriend and in a different environment, his personality improved. I was beginning to think he was getting well—wrong!

Things went well for a while. It was during the time of the Patty Hearst disappearance. I remember this because she had been seen in the Havasu area.

Bill got a job as a draftsman for the City of Havasu. I found a temporary job at the radio station in Havasu. It was right up my alley and I liked it a lot. But, it was only a temporary position. I only worked there for approximately a month.

Again, Bill's personality began to change dramatically. I never knew what he would be like when he would get home from work, and it was hell. I told him I wanted to drive across country to see my sister in Alexandria, Virginia, and he was okay with it. I was thinking, then, that I might not come back. Women should always listen to their intuition.

I called my brother, Herman, and he flew out to Phoenix, Arizona and I picked him up at the airport and we drove across country together. It was a good time for us to spend some time together, because it had been so long since I had seen him. We drove straight through. He would drive while I slept, then I would drive while he slept. We would stop at gas stations to use the bathroom and clean up a little. We made the trip in three days.

It was good to see my sister, Jo, and her family! I stayed in Alexandria for a few weeks. I even got a temporary job in Washington, DC, through Kelly Girl Services. This was a way to make some quick money.

Bill kept calling me and asking me when I plan to return home. I said I didn't know but was thinking I might stay in Virginia. Then, one day he called and said a preacher's wife in Havasu had asked him if I could pick up his wife in Missouri on my return home.

Jo did not want me to go back after I had told her the things that had been going on, but now I felt obligated to pick up the preacher's wife in Missouri (another bad decision). I returned, driving back across the USA, not knowing what I would go back to. The drive went well and I did go by Missouri and returned the preacher's wife to her home in Havasu.

After returning, Bill was worse than ever; I regretted coming back to this! I found a job as receptionist at a construction company in Havasu. I liked all the people I worked with and felt very happy with my job. It seemed the happier I became with my job, the more jealous and mean he would become.

I called Paul and explained to him what was going on and asked if he could send me $200 to help me get away when I decided to. He said he would but that I was to put it in the bank and not touch it until I needed it to go. He sent me $200 and I opened a bank account. I felt good knowing I could leave this man at any time I needed.

I had finally had enough of his mental abuse and decided to leave him. On a Friday afternoon after I got off of work, I did not go home. I went to my girlfriend's home in Havasu to stay for the weekend, trying to figure out what I wanted to do; also the banks weren't open until Monday. It was so peaceful not being around him. I should have known my actions wouldn't fly with him.

I had talked to my girlfriend and the estimator at the company about Bill's behavior. So they were aware of it and they were watching out for me.

As a receptionist in the company, all the calls would come through me, and each time that Bill would call, someone else would answer the call. They kept a gun in their desk drawer, at all times. On Monday, instead of calling, Bill just came up to my work on his Yamaha and opened the door and there I sat. I saw the estimator reach in his desk and I looked at him and shook my head.

Bill said, "Get home right now!" I got up to leave and they looked at me and said, "Call us if you need us, okay?" I nodded. On the way home, while sitting on the back of his motor bike, I was praying, *"God, please get me out of this and I promise I will get away from him and do better."* (Of course, it was under my breath.)

When we got home, Bill went around and closed all the window shades and doors and came toward me with a weird look on his face. I thought I was going to die, for sure! He began asking me where I had been and I told him I had stayed at my girlfriend's house and that I was not happy being here with him any longer. He came toward me and began to strike at me, but I was catching his fist with my arms.

He did get one hit on my forehead, until I began screaming at him, "You woman beater, why don't you pick on a man! You only hit on women, you coward!"

He stopped and just looked at me and said, "I am so sorry!" I just stood there and glared at him, most likely showing my hatred for him. He kept apologizing, and just then, the phone rang. It was the estimator at work asking me how things were going. I said okay and he hung up. They were all worried about me.

I never went back to work there because I had plans. I would have been too embarrassed to face any of them anyway. I did stay in touch with the estimator and my girlfriend.

In the meantime, he was trying to get me a position at his work. It would be helping him in the drafting department. They asked me to come in, and after talking with the manager I got the job. I was to begin work the following week. I had no intention of staying around much longer and no intention of ever going to work there, especially since I had prayed to God that if he would get me out of this a few days earlier, I would leave. I just went through the motion until I could work it out.

He had an appointment to go to Phoenix for a real estate exam on the upcoming Friday and I had already made up my mind as soon as he left that I would be leaving and heading back up to Oregon. I felt that was the only choice I had.

He left early in the morning, and as soon as I heard his truck leave, I jumped out of bed, showered, and threw my clothes in the car, along with photos and belongings I did not want to leave behind.

I called my girlfriend, Sue, whom I had met in Azusa to let her know that I would be coming through West Covina. She asked me to stay with her overnight and then leave for Oregon the following morning. I headed away of Havasu, after stopping by the bank and withdrawing the $200.

While driving across the desert, my heart was racing and trying not to speed, thinking that he might be following me. Thank God, the road was flat and I could see for miles. I headed out as fast as possible and never looked back.

I was happy to be leaving in my yellow "Bic Banana" car. That's what I called it; I had traded my little green car for it. It was a yellow Torino with a black top.

When I arrived in West Covina, I felt safe. It was good to have a calm place to settle down a bit prior to driving the long distance to Oregon. I, kiddingly, blamed Sue for the mess I was in. She said she never knew that side of him. If she had she would have never suggested my going out with him.

Early the next morning, I left early for Shingletown. I drove for ten hours, and on the way up the long I-5 Corridor I felt so helpless and all I could do was to pray, *"Lord, please show me the way. I've really messed up my life and don't know where to go or what to do. My life is in your hands."* It was one of the longest trips I've ever made and always wondering if he would be on my trail.

CHAPTER 21

ON JULY 10, 1973, I arrived at the home of Alice and Leonard, in Shingletown. They had no way of knowing that I was coming. They were excited and glad to see me. Finally, I had gotten away from this crazy guy and back with my family! It was dinner time and I felt so welcomed and safe with them.

I could only think that I had really messed up my life and what was I to do, now? I wanted to find work ASAP and I began job hunting, right away.

Leonard taught music at the local schools. He is so talented, and can play any instrument, along with being an artist. He also did gigs in the local places, like Shakey's Pizza and the Elks Club. We would go watch him play and have dinner.

He tried to teach Alice and me how to play the guitar in his class, but I felt my hands weren't large enough to reach the cords. I also wanted to learn faster than he was teaching—didn't take it serious! Wish I had had the patience.

One week after I arrived, Alice, some friends, and I were at the Hilton in Redding. A gentleman kept asking us to dance and he kept going back and forth from our table to the bar. I finally asked him why he kept going back to the bar and he said that his friend was up there. I said, "What is your friend's name?" He said his name was Jack.

After a couple of drinks and being relaxed, I yelled out across the bar, "J A C K!" That's when Jack turned around and we motioned for him to come over to our table. (This would stop his friend from running back and forth.) I never realized how this particular night would change my life.

We made a long night of eating, drinking, dancing and getting to know them both. Jack's friend owned a beauty school in Redding. He and Jack were the best of friends and they played tennis together. Jack's soon to be ex-wife was a model at his friend's beauty school. Jack was an appraiser for the City of Redding. He and his wife were going through a separation at that time. The last thing I was looking for, at this time, was to meet another man—especially, a married man just separating from his wife!

I had been thinking while driving all the way back up to Shingletown from Havasu that I might return to North Carolina and that I had made a terrible mistake in leaving in the first place. As they've always said, "Things happen when you least expect it!"

A few days went by and Jack came by and asked me to go have coffee with him the next day. I did meet him the next morning and we talked for a long time. This would be the beginning of a very long relationship.

A few weeks later, my sister and I had driven down to Redding and when we arrived back up the hill to her house. Her son, Dean, came running out of the driveway yelling, "He's here, he's here!" They all had been told to be on the watch for Bill, my ex-boyfriend. He told us that the crazy one had come to the house looking for me.

Alice told me to drop her off and get the heck back down the hill to a friend's home. Joe was a good friend of Alice and Leonard. Joe and Leonard were away on a trip to the Oregon Coast to fish. Joe had invited us to stay at his house while he was away. We were going back up the hill only to pick up more clothing.

I hurriedly dropped her off and headed back down the hill. They had two ways to get to their home from Redding, so I took the least travelled road back. I immediately put my car in Joe's garage so it couldn't be seen and waited for her to come back down the hill. My yellow car could be spotted a mile away; I felt safe having it in an enclosed garage.

When she arrived back to Joe's home, she told me that she had met with him (we began to call him "crazy Willy"), at a service station up in Shingletown, and had spoken with him. She told him that I did not want to be with him anymore and that I had driven up to Oregon.

He didn't believe what she was saying, however, she convinced him that I wasn't in the area. She also said that he had a look on his face that would kill! She said he looked crazy in the head and his eyes were just wild. She felt that if I had met with him, he would have surely killed me! (He must have been off his medications.)

When Joe and Leonard came back from the Oregon Coast, I left Joe's home and got a room at the motel and left my car in Joe's garage (with his approval of course).

Even though Jack and I were keeping our relationship low-key until his divorce was final, he asked me to go to San Francisco with him. I loved the idea because I could get away from Redding and thinking that "crazy Willy" could still be around there looking for me. Sure enough, as we were going down the I-5, heading for San Francisco, we passed his truck heading back up toward Redding. Jack was driving his 1955 Mercedes and I felt safe knowing he wouldn't recognize me in Jack's car.

I called Alice's friend when I arrived in San Francisco to let Alice know to be on the lookout for "crazy Willy" and to please not to let him know where I was, if she did see him and to stay safe.

Jack and I spent the weekend in San Francisco and we had a wonderful time. It was one of the best times that I had had in a very long time. Jack was a total gentleman, and we got along great. While we were at Coit Tower; offering a 360 degree of the city and bay, "helpful Henry" (he called me) locked us out of his car, thinking he had the keys in his pocket. He had to use his belt buckle to open the lock through an open window. When it came time to leave, I did not want to go back to Shingletown, and reality set in.

While I was away, Alice had not heard from "crazy Willy" at all. That was a relief! We all felt he had returned to Southern California by this time.

Finally, my job hunting paid off! Several positions were offered and I had my pick of them; one was at a dental office as a dental assistant. (The dentist would train me.) I was excited about this one. I had purchased my uniforms and had one more interview before beginning work. However, when I got to my last interview, the dentist made me feel very uncomfortable with his suggestive comments.

I saw photos of his wife and children on his desk and asked him, "Don't you think your wife would be upset with you if she heard you talking this way?" He was telling me how attractive I was and came toward me as if he was going to kiss me. I quickly grabbed my purse and got out of his office.

I can still see the look on his receptionists face! She probably knew him and understood what was happening. Later, I learned that he had been this way with other women applying for work. I am thankful I did not to take that position.

The other positions were at the high school's superintendent's office, and at a telephone company. After evaluating the two positions, I picked the telephone company. I was very excited and couldn't wait to begin work.

About a month later, I received a letter from the estimator at the construction company in Havasu, inquiring how I was doing. He wrote, "It's too bad what Bill did!" I had no idea what he was saying in his letter. Since Alice and Leonard did not have a phone, I had to wait until I could get down to a pay phone to call him to see what he was referring to in his letter.

When we did get down to Redding, I found a phone and called him to ask him what he was referring to in his letter. He said, "You didn't know?" I told him I didn't know anything because I had stayed away from him, altogether. He said that he had killed himself, by a self inflicted gunshot wound. I could hardly believe my ears! Alice saw me shaking and upset and took the phone and talked with him a bit prior to hanging up.

I was so upset and of course blamed myself for what he had done. When Jack saw me later, I told him what had happened and he and I went to a restaurant and lounge and he was so good at comforting me. He had once been a counselor and knew exactly how to handle my emotions. He kept reminding me that it wasn't my fault, and he just let me cry. Thank God I had a true friend to help me through this difficult time!

If there was any good to come out of this tragedy, it was that now we wouldn't have to worry about "crazy Willy" ever coming into our lives again, and causing us problems. It look a long time for me to forget about his death and the memories, good and bad, but eventually, with Jack's help, I was able to let it go.

I had my job; now I had to find a place to live. There was a girl who worked with me who was looking for a roommate. She asked me to move in with her in an A-frame home on the Sacramento River in Downtown Redding.

(A-frame on the Sacramento River)

(Alice and Leonard at my A-Frame)

This would be convenient for me because I didn't have as far to travel to work and it was close to all the amenities. She and I would lay in our twin beds upstairs and look out over the Sacramento River and watch the ducks and other waterfowl swim by and we would talk for hours. Our home was facing the west, so we had fabulous views of the Trinity Mountains and the sunsets of Redding. The A-frame was small but it was just the right size for the two of us.

I fell asleep one night, after my roommate and I had been talking, and I had a dream about Bill (crazy Willy). It was so clear; I saw him standing in front of me and he said to me, *"I am sorry for the way I treated you and don't blame yourself for my taking my own life. It was not your fault. I was just screwed up!"* I was so shocked when I awaken, knowing that he had visited me in my sleep to help me go on with my life, and not to blame myself for his death.

By this time, I had gotten a phone. A few days later, I received a call that sounded like an elderly lady and when I said hello, she said, "J-e-r-r-i-e!" The phone went dead. All I could think of was that it was Bill's grandma trying to reach me. She sounded like she was crying? I never tried to reach her and I never heard from her again.

I had finally gotten to the point where I felt it was time to have my children back with me. I was missing them so much and it was leaving a void in my life.

In the meantime, Jack's wife was in the process of moving out of their home because she was going to move in with her boyfriend. Her boyfriend had been living there with her, but they wanted to move out into a place of their own.

Jack was still making the payments on his home and he asked me if I wanted to move into it and help with the payments. Of course, I thought it would be perfect for me and the children (as soon as they came back from North Carolina). His home was a four-bedroom home and it was located in the country-club area of Redding. I was very happy to have the opportunity to live there.

My roommate was okay with my leaving the A-frame, too, because she was planning to move to Reno, Nevada, to become a card dealer. It seemed everything was working out just fine.

I called Paul to let him know that I had found a home and had a good job and things were going well and that I was ready to have the children come back to me. He agreed, and sent them back on an airplane. We had to all stay in the A-frame until Jack's wife had moved out of their home, however. The A-frame was cramped with my room-mate, me, and my three children, but it was great having my children back with me again and these close quarters didn't last very long.

I had met Jack in July, 1973, one week after I arrived in Redding. My three children and I moved into his home the end of August, 1973. The same day that Jack's wife moved out of their home, I moved in. The neighbors must have really wondered what was going on at this house. We had very nice neighbors and they had children the same ages as mine, which was good for my children. It was a safe and nice area of Redding. It seemed that God had answered all my prayers.

(Jack and My first photo together [1973])

Jack was living with his parents, who lived just around the corner from us. He felt it would be a good idea for me to live in his house, so that when his kids came to visit him we could all be together.

Jack was an avid tennis player at the Redding Country Club, and would spend much of his spare time playing tennis. I would become frustrated with him because that seemed to be his main interest. I would say to him, "You are the happiest when you are with your country club friends."

I would see a change in him, sometimes, when he would be gone most of the weekend over at the country club. I became jealous of some of the women because he would sometimes compare me with them. It got to the point that I didn't even want to go over there and I began to resent them.

However, one evening, we went over for a dance and while we were dancing, one of the ladies came up to me and hugged us both and said, "Jack, you have picked a winner!" This gave me more confidence in myself and I eventually opened up to them and we became friends. I came to realize that just because they attended the country club didn't mean they were snobbish. They became very good friends to me and we would have many get togethers and dinners and playing tennis together.

With me coming from a small town and being sheltered most of my life, I had not really had an opportunity to experience an upscale society atmosphere such as this. Jack liked the finer things in life and some people would mistake him for being cold and snoody at times. Jack was a quiet man and was vain with his looks. Although, he had a heart of gold and would do anything for anyone.

He knew a lot of people in the Redding area because he had lived there most of his life. He graduated from Shasta High School in Redding and his class was the first to attend Shasta College and his class even gave it it's name, colors, and mascot.

It had been seven years since I had left North Carolina and I still had not gotten my divorce from Paul. Jack was thinking more seriously about our relationship and asked me to go ahead and get my divorce finalized. I was glad that I had not gotten my divorce because it kept me single and gave me a good excuse not to marry again; since Bill had wanted us to marry. I wasn't ready still, at this point, and I was not sure about another marriage. It was beginning to seem that one day Jack and my relationship would be fine and the next day we would be arguing about something. I would go to work and talk with my friends and they would say, "You two will never make it!" We had a rocky relationship in the beginning. To be honest, I never felt we would make it either, but there was something about him that I didn't want to lose.

CHAPTER 22

MY MOVING INTO his house was good timing because it was just before the school year began. The children loved it and had many playmates and the streets were always full of kids and dogs running around, playing basketball, and riding their bikes. We lived on the end of a cul-de-sac, which made it safer for the children.

Jack's children where already familiar with the area and they had gained many friends and weren't real happy about having to move out of the area with their mother. Jack's daughter, Debby, and his two sons, John and Dan, moved into an apartment with their mother and her boyfriend.

Jack's oldest son, John, wasn't happy living with his mother and her boyfriend. He wasn't shy in saying so, either. He once told Jack that her boyfriend had grabbed him and threatened to hit him. Jack became so angry that he went over to their apartment and told him that if he ever laid another hand on his son he would punch him out. Jack was 6 feet tall, with a slender built, and in very good shape. Her boyfriend was a much smaller and shorter man and he seemed to be intimidated. He also had the "little man" mentality.

John wasn't adjusting to his mother's living arrangement and asked his dad if he could come live with me. We agreed it was a good idea for John, since his closest friends lived in the neighborhood and the school was only a couple of blocks from our home. John came to live with me and my children and things went well with the two families adjusting.

Later, after Jack's wife and her boyfriend split up, we read in the newspaper that his present girlfriend's child had been murdered. It was never determined what happened to the child, and I don't think anyone was ever convicted of it. But, we felt that was too close to home, so to speak. We were glad that he was no longer acquainted with Jack's children.

It was convenient for us to walk around the corner to his parents' home to visit. We would go over there for dinner and they would come over to my home for dinner. The arrangement seemed to be great for us all.

(Me with Jack and his mother, Anne)

My home was sparsely decorated, coming from a small A-frame home. We had to wait until I began receiving my paychecks before we could begin buying furniture and a washer and dryer. After returning from the laundry mat, one evening, just as I opened the front door, I noticed my back slider door was open and the curtains were moving in the breeze. I immediately told all the children to get back in the car and I reach in and got the wall phone to call Jack (while standing outside the door). I told him that someone had been or may still be in the house and that things had been thrown all over the floor and the slider was still open!

A few minutes later, Jack came driving up through our backyard (in case the intruder[s] had run out the backdoor). We checked around the house and found the intruders had come in through a window in my son's bedroom and had left foot tracks all the way down the hall-way. Our movies, VCR tapes, and records had been thrown all over the living room floor and some were missing. Also, I found later that they had taken a roast that was in the freezer! They must have been hungry robbers! It was a sloppy job and seemed it was most likely kids.

This incident made me nervous to stay there alone because I kept thinking the intruders would come back. So, Jack stayed overnight that night. After we were all asleep, my daughter came running up the hall, saying, "There's someone trying to break in to the house!" We were already on edge!

We all got up and began looking around the entire home, but nothing was found out of place. Then, suddenly, we heard a noise that rumbled throughout the home. It did sound like someone was trying to break in.

Jack called the police and we all sat in a huddle until they arrived. The noise stopped. The police checked out all around the house and after we told them what had happened earlier, they took prints from the window that had been broken into. We filed a report with them and they left and went on their way after nothing was found.

Just as we were about to go back to bed, the noise began again; it seemed even louder than before. Our adrenalin kicked in again and we began checking throughout the house again. Finally, we determined that the noise was coming from the attic. Jack got on the ladder and looked in it and the noise stopped. We then realized it must be "roof rats," (that's what they called those little critters in Redding) and they were very common in the area because of all the vegetation around the homes.

The next morning we called the exterminator, and after he came out he found a small mouse with its tail caught in a trap. He must have been running around the attic stuck in the trap and banging against the rafters. It was funny later but it wasn't so funny at the time! Jack went back over to his parents' home the next morning and everything went back to normal.

School began and the children were back in school. It was convenient, because while I was at work the children were old enough to walk home from school and stay by themselves until I arrived home from work and since John being the oldest, was able to be there with the younger ones.

They all attended the same school that Jack's brother was once the principle of, and everyone there knew the "Duckett" name. They did very well in school and liked all of their teachers; they still mention them and talk about that school.

My daughter, Paula, was a good runner and she beat the school's record in running. The very next year, she beat her previous year's record. She was told she ran like a racehorse—very straight and steady.

Jack's other two children remained with his wife and her new boyfriend. She'd had a few car accidents before and Jack was always afraid for Dan and Debby to ride with her. He never understood why she would have so many accidents. He would say that she was careless and unaware of her surroundings.

My son, Rick, was having problems at school and trouble adjusting because John was older than him and Dan was younger and he was in the middle of the two. It seemed each time anything would happen, he would get the blame. He was beginning to act up in school and his grades were dropping. It was getting so bad that I called Paul and we decided that Rick would be better off living with him in North Carolina. It was hard for me, but I had to think of my son, first. Having to live with a mixed family was taking its toll on us all. We felt Rick needed his dad with his sports and schooling to help him grow into a stable and healthy young man. So, we flew Rick out to North Carolina to live with his dad.

Jack and his wife finalized their divorce and she was allotted the 1955 Mercedes in the divorce, along with all the furniture and savings account. Jack took all the bills, house, and the other car, a BMW, because she couldn't make the payments.

I went to court and got my final divorce papers signed by the Judge and they were forwarded to Paul for his signature. Paul and I were divorced after seven years of separation.

Jack was an appraiser for Shasta County, and while driving around Redding one day he saw the 1955 Mercedes, "Bam" (that was his license plate), parked at a service station; it had been wrecked. The passenger side window was cracked. He was terrified, and upon calling his ex, he found out that Dan's head had hit the window. After seeing the car, Jack was concerned that something terrible had happened to Dan. He found out that Dan had only a small knot on his forehead. This made him more concern about him riding with her.

Jack's ex-wife had remarried, and was living in Shingletown. The marriage lasted only a short time and while they were in the process of getting a divorce, her husband asked her to remove his last name. She went back to the name of Duckett. Debby had written in her diary about events happening at her mother's house and Jack did not think a teenage girl should be around it (parties, drinking, etc.). Debby would tell us other things, too, that would upset Jack. He was concerned about them both being with their mother.

By this time, Jack and I were living together and Debby had spent the weekend with us. It was July 24, 1977, when Jack, Debby, and I went up to Alice's home in Shingletown to a Garage sale. She and Leonard were moving to Hawaii and they were liquidating all their assets. It was fun checking everything out and we even purchased a few small items. Debby really wanted to purchase a coat that Alice was selling and we told her we would come back later and get it for her, because it was the end of the day and we didn't think it would sell, thinking we could get it cheaper. Although, we felt Debby didn't really need it, anyway. Debby met up with her mother at the garage sale and Jack and I left to go back down the hill to Redding.

The following morning, I was at work and it was 10 a.m., on July 25, 1977, when I received a call from Jack. He could hardly talk. He was crying and saying, "Debby is dead!" I looked out my office window and saw him sitting out front in his car. I ran out and told him to get out from under the wheel and I drove as fast as possible over to his parents. I told Jack's mother that Debby had been killed in a car wreck while she and her mother were driving down the hill from Shingletown to work and school. His mother almost collapsed and began screaming and running into her bedroom. Jack followed her, trying to console her. His dad came into the house wondering what in the world was happening!

Debby was killed at the Bear Creek Bridge, located on Highway 44. She was only seventeen years of age. The area of the wreck is also where mine and Alice's children had played and swam many times. It was a very curvy and steep highway from Shingletown to Redding.

People had stated that they had seen the car speeding by at a high rate of speed. To this day, no one really knows who was driving because both of them were thrown from the vehicle. The car had rolled over Debby's head. Debby's shoes were knocked completely off her feet, but had remained in the car.

(Debby's Gravesite in Redding)

Debby's mother was in a coma in the Redding Memorial Hospital for over a month. She never seemed, mentally, to be the same again. She had also lost her spleen and had some internal injuries. Eventually, she was released from the hospital, but still remained under doctor's care.

Jack's mother had gone up to check the car out after the accident and found Dan's jacket lying in the backseat. She took the jacket and held on to it so Jack wouldn't see it. She knew how Jack felt about having Dan ride with his mother. Dan could have easily been in the car but he was staying with his maternal grandparents at the time of the accident.

Jack and I made up our minds that we were going to court to get custody of Dan, particularly now that this had happened. Jack called her parents to ask when they were going to bring Dan back to him and they responded, "Never!" Jack said, "We will see about that!"

We had a close friend who was a judge at that time and we began filling out papers to get custody of him. The judge, however, had to disqualify himself from the case because of his relationship with Jack. They were close friends and would play tennis and jog together in the mornings.

It took several months for everything to be approved, but after being interviewed several times by child psychologists we finally got the custody. His ex's parents had court orders to hand Dan over to us. He came to live with us and had visitation rights with his mother, but he was not to ride with her when she was driving.

Dan's mother married for the third time and she moved to Susanville, California. We had full custody of Dan, but we allowed him to go spend time with his mother and her new husband whenever they would ask for him.

Jack was an excellent tennis player and would play in tennis tournaments all around Redding and throughout the states of California and Oregon. We enjoyed travelling and watching him play in the tournaments on the weekends. His career allowed him the freedom to do it during the week, at times.

His job as appraiser was dissolved when California's Proposition 13 took effect. He had been employed with Shasta County for fourteen years. He knew he had to find another career, and after several months as a contractor completing appraisals with several banks, he found a position with MARTA in Atlanta, Georgia.

He would travel back and forth from Redding to Atlanta (coming home on weekends). After working there for a couple of months, they offered him a full-time position. We planned to move back to Atlanta, but still had a lot of items to take care of. I began looking for work back there, too, and had an interview set up.

In the meantime, Paula had asked if she could go back to live in North Carolina to go to school with her brother, just until we moved back to Georgia. I thought it would be good for her to be with her brother. Paul and I talked and he agreed. Paula and I boarded a plane back to Atlanta, where Paul and his new wife picked her up at the Atlanta airport and I met Jack there and spent a couple of days with him prior to my returning to Redding.

Jack was unhappy with his job in Atlanta and felt like a minority in the company. He wasn't accustomed to being the only Caucasian in an all African American business. He eventually gave up his job and the idea of moving to Georgia, so he came home.

CHAPTER 23

IN JULY OF 1978, Jack and I decided we should get married; we had been living together for four years. It appeared we were married, anyway.

He had never been back to the South, but we had talked about it many times. We thought it would be a good idea to get married in South Carolina and stay at Hilton Head Island after our wedding. We had always wanted to visit Hilton Head. I called and made reservations and then called the courthouse in the little town outside of Hilton Head named Ridgeland, South Carolina. We set the date of August 11, 1978, and were married by the judge at Ridgeland Courthouse.

(Jack and me in front of the Courthouse in Ridgeland, South Carolina)

Pam was back in North Carolina for the summer. We flew to Hilton Head and John and Dan were our witnesses.

Our marriage was on the weekend and we couldn't find a jewelry store open, so we bought a ring at the drugstore to use at the ceremony. It was an inexpensive ring with a cross and flowers around it.

We found a turquoise band to use for Jack. It was a short and sweet wedding.

(Jack and Me after our wedding)

When we returned home, his parents were upset with us for not telling them that we were getting married. We hadn't told anyone, because it had been such a spontaneous decision. I hadn't even told my own children. It felt good being married again and beginning a brand new life as a married couple.

Jack was becoming unhappy with his travelling contracting jobs and wanted to find a full-time position. He heard they were hiring in Alaska for a position at the department of transportation. He called and set up an interview and we flew to Juneau, Alaska.

As we were flying into Juneau it was one of the most beautiful sites I had ever seen. The white glacier was sparkling with different shades of blue and the mountains were covered with snow. The fields were in bloom with beautiful purple and yellow wildflowers.

When we arrived, it was such a quaint little town, with narrow streets. The waterfront had large cruise ships docked. I was so excited when I saw one of them disembark and I wondered if they spoke English or a foreign language since it was a Greek ship and the workers were speaking a foreign language. I went up to ask a passenger where they were from and she said they were from Los Angeles, California. I had to laugh.

We had reservations at the old hotel downtown, in Juneau, Alaska called the Baranof Hotel. It was like going back in time because of its age, décor, and history. After our trip to Juneau, the hotel burned down completely. I am so glad that we had the opportunity to stay there with its nostalgia, beforehand.

We were sitting out on the pier at 11 p.m. and it was still daylight. It was so beautiful. We would sit and watch the cruise ships depart. I had never really realized how large they were! The moon was out, even though it was still daylight.

(Cruise ship in Juneau)

We had an opportunity to walk down to the glacier the next day and it was really neat to have all that ice around us and it was as warm as a summer's day. The waters in the streams looked like milk coming off the glacier. The ferns were taller than we were and I felt like I was in the land of the giants. I will never forget how I felt with all that beauty around us.

(Mendenhall Glacier, Juneau, Alaska)

Jack went to his interview and it went well, but they told him that he would need to go to Anchorage to meet with another official for the final decision. We boarded a plane to Anchorage, Alaska. Of course, we didn't have a reservation. There were no rooms available but we did rent a car (at least we had a roof over our heads).

We would stop at different hotels and Jack would tell me to go inside to see if anything was available. We were getting weary because nightfall was coming and we were getting desperate. When I went into the Hilton, they said they didn't have any rooms. I must have looked like I was beginning to cry because the clerk looked at me and said, "Don't cry." He then said, "We do have one of the old rooms called the 'sourdough' rooms. If you would like to see them, I will show it to you." He showed it to me and I was so grateful! It was clean, but it was an old room that looked like it was used many, many years ago by the fishermen. All we needed was a place to lay our heads for the night.

When I went back to the car to tell Jack that we had a room, he was relieved and asked me what I did to get it; smiling. I told him I was close to tears and they felt sorry for me.

The next day, it was late in the day when he got to his interview. He said it went very well and we were excited that he had a good chance of getting the job and we might be moving to Alaska! We loved the Juneau area.

Since it was so late in the day, however, we had to get a room for another night. So, I went back to the front desk and they had a room available on the seventh floor. It was beautiful and overlooked Anchorage.

The next day we had a little time to spend before our flight left, so we drove down the peninsula to do some sightseeing. It was a dreary day and kind of scary for us since we had heard about the tides they have there. The tides can come in so quickly that you could be stranded in a flash if you were down near the water. So, we just stayed in the car. I was exhausted and ready to leave when it came time for our flight.

Unfortunately, Jack did not get the job at the Department of Transportation in Alaska; they hired from within.

When we returned from Alaska, my daughter, Pam, said she wanted to change her last name to Duckett. She said she would feel better with everyone else's last name. It wasn't legally changed, but she did change her name to Duckett on all her school papers. Now, she felt more like a member of the Duckett family.

Jack's father, Johnny, passed away in September, 1978. He had been ill for a while and had been hospitalized. He was one of the nicest men I had ever known. He loved Jack's mother so much and would do anything for her. His whole world turned around her. He also loved my children and they thought the world of him. I would cut his hair and he would always be so appreciative. He was such a nice man.

He was buried in Redding cemetery, next to Debby's grave. After his death, Jack had to help his mother many times, doing things for her that Johnny would have done around the house. I tried to help a lot, too, with the yard, keeping it raked and cleaned up.

His mother, Anne, had emphysema and had to wear an oxygen apparatus 24/7. She was progressively getting worse and worse. But, she continued to smoke and it irritated Jack. She would come over to our home and sit by the kitchen stove with the Jenn-Aire vent running, holding her cigarette over it. He had finally had enough and one night, she said, "Do you mind if I smoke?" Jack replied, "Yes, I mind. . . I don't like to sit and watch you kill yourself!" They would go for weeks at a time without speaking to each other when one would get irritated with the other one. They were a lot alike.

Anne had a mind of her own and no one could tell her what to do but she and I got along great. The kids and I would go over and play cards (her favorite pastime) with her and she would usually win. She I would spend a lot of time together while Jack was away. I would take the children over there for dinner and she would come over to see us. She was a wonderful seamstress and loved to sew outfits for me. We would sit and talk about anything and everything. She became a true friend to me.

Jack and I did a lot of travelling together. We loved Hawaii, and we visited the Big Island of Hawaii, and Maui. We also enjoyed visiting many areas of Mexico.

(Me in Hawaii)

After visiting Mexico, we decided Mexico seemed to have a lot more to offer than Hawaii. We took several trips there and really got to know a lot about the country. We looked at real estate several times and had a realtor keep us informed as to the market and called us on many of them. The only thing that kept us from purchasing a home in Puerto Vallarta was finding out that the state owns the property.

(Me and Jack at the Sea of Cortez, Mexico)

(View from our villa in Zihuatanejo, Mexico)

It was stressful for Jack, having to always be away on his job and missing out on birthdays, events, and sometimes holidays. He had to go where the money was and each time he would leave, he would wonder when he would be home again. He travelled all over the United States. I was fortunate to have had the opportunity to go meet him at times.

He was away on business so often that I decided to get involved with the BPW (Business and Professional Women) organization. We would give fashion shows to raise money and I would model for them at fashion shows. One of my girlfriends, Trish, and I had fun doing this modeling. I also learned public speaking and this really helped in my career.

I was also able to get out and meet other ladies and make new friends.

(Me modeling at one of BPW'S fashion Shows)

Jack took no responsibility for things around the house, such as the yard, home repairs, etc. He wasn't good at keeping records of his travelling expenses, either. It was all I could do with keeping up with our home, my job, the checking account, paying the bills, making sure the taxes were completed, making sure the money was in the bank to cover his credit card expenses and taking care of the children.

When I went to get our taxes completed, I was told that we owed $14,000 in taxes! I was taken back so much that I took them to another lady, who had once worked for the IRS, and she completed them and saved us $7,000! I told the original tax man I wasn't going to pay him for his service because of his mistake, and I didn't pay him. We paid the IRS what was due. I never want to be on the wrong side of the IRS!

I was admitted to the hospital for surgery (hysterectomy) and my daddy came out to California for a visit, saying he would help me after my surgery. It was helpful having him there and I enjoyed seeing him again; it had been such a long time since I had seen him. The last time I had seen him was when Ricky was a baby and we were visiting Jo and Carl in 1966. Ricky was cutting teeth and crying and daddy said, "That kid has to go, or I will." I said, "It looks like you will because he isn't going anywhere." He left the next morning.

Daddy soon moved in with my brother, Herman, who was now living in Anderson, California, a few miles from us and had a single-wide trailer. He remained with Herman for a while until moving into a room at a hotel in downtown.

I would go visit him, occasionally, and then he would come over to our home for dinner and would help me in the yard with landscaping. Once, I overheard him talking while he was working out in the yard and I asked him who was he talking to and he said he was talking to himself. I said, "That is okay, as long as you don't begin answering yourself." He was beginning to get senile. I really enjoyed our last days together. I would look at him and wonder how and why he gave us children so much grief when we were young. There was nothing "scary" about him, now being a little old man! I was feeling compassion for him.

He would get real dizzy and have to quit working and have to sit. I was beginning to worry about him. He was still drinking, and Jack didn't want him coming around when he was drinking. I seldom saw him sober. I was beginning to feel real pity for this man. He was living in one room in an older hotel in Redding. There were a lot of misfits (as they appeared), and people with no families living there. He would get food from the food bank and try to give some of it to us, but I would tell him to keep it; we didn't need it. He would store it under his bed. Daddy did have a heart and he would give anything he had away if someone asked for it. Unfortunately, I never saw this in him when I was a child.

Daddy would tell me many times how proud he was of me as an adult and how much he respected me for graduating from school and having a good job and doing well. I enjoyed feeling that I had made my daddy proud.

He gave me the only money he had ($400) and ask me to put it in the bank and save it for him because he didn't know how to save money. I did deposit it and in a couple of months he came over and asked me for the money because he wanted to buy an airline ticket and go back to North Carolina. He left the West Coast and went to live with my sister, Pat.

Jack's son, John, graduated from high school and remained living with us for a while. I had always been an avid NASCAR fan and John became interested in racing. He got a race car and began racing at Shasta Speedway in Redding. Once, while Jack was away on business, John, his friends and I were out by the pool and drinking wine together. We decided we would like to drive John's race car around the neighborhood. So, we all took turns driving it throughout the neighborhood. We made sure that the youngest child, Danny, would drive it (so he wouldn't mention it to Jack)! Someone came over to tell us that our neighbor had called the police. We hurriedly put the race car in the garage and ran inside. The policeman came and knocked on our door. John told us all to be quiet and he went to the door. The policeman asked who was driving a race car and John told him that we didn't know anything about it. Everyone was so quiet and calm that the policeman believed us and left. We laughed, realizing that we had gotten away with it! It was worth it. We had such a good time. Jack never knew of this incident until years later.

John was hired at the same telephone company where I was

working, as a mailroom carrier. He continued his education, attending Shasta College, and got his degree. He was promoted up to our accounting department. He did so well he was soon promoted to Accounting Manager. He continued his education, going to night school. Eventually, he moved out of our home and married. He is now the City of Shasta's city manager, and doing very well. He has two sons.

Things were beginning to change with my and Jack's relationship. He would come home with an attitude that caused me to wonder what was up with him. Of course he would always say it was my fault. Maybe I was getting a little independent? I would get so upset with him and so tired of his actions that I wouldn't want him to come home, and I suppose he felt the same way. We began to argue more and were growing further and further apart.

In the meantime, I was still taking care of our children and continuing to work five days a week. I began to think it was a losing battle. We talked about our relationship many times, but he would always say it was me and not him who had changed and then he would go away, again.

He would leave at times, saying, "I want you out of here by the time I get back!" It would hurt so much to hear this, but I knew I had to take care of the children, with their needs. I never knew whether he really meant it or not, and didn't even know if I should stay married to him or not.

Once, while he was at home, I received a phone call from a woman in Dallas, Texas, wanting to know if she could talk with Jack. I asked who was calling and she said, "A friend." He talked with her, laughing and talking. When he hung up I asked him who it was and he said, "I can't believe she called me. She is someone I met when we played basketball with a few people down in Texas." I said, didn't sound like a casual conversation." That ended our conversation.

When he left on his next trip, he asked Danny, Pam, and me to fly down to Burbank, California, to meet up with him. We flew down and he seemed happy to see us. Pam and Danny went to the pool to swim one afternoon and Jack and I stayed in the room. He got a call and his face went pale and he just stared at me. After he hung up, I asked him who it was and what was wrong and he told me that it was the bartender at the motel (a lady). He said she had asked him, "Are you cheating on me?"

I became so upset and told him I was going down to the bar to see this woman! He tried to stop me, but I went down and looked her in the eyes and asked, "What is your game?" She told me that the guy who was working with Jack had put her up to it and it was just a joke. I told her, "It may be a joke to you, but it's not a joke to me!" She apologized.

In my anger, I was ready to leave at that moment to go back home, but Jack convinced me that it was a joke and he promised me he had been true to me, all along. I was beginning to put two and two together, and failed to really believe him but let it go.

Upon our return home, things were quickly going downhill between us. I was happy to see him leave and I knew he wanted to go.

I began thinking I was single and acting like it. I would go out with my girlfriends for dinner, dancing and acting single. I was thinking he was doing the same. But, of course, he always was telling me he was being faithful to me. I would also go out on houseboats, partying and going to the bars. I wasn't real happy in what I felt I was being forced to do.

I do admit that I had a short affair with a man from work. He was married and I knew it would never last. But, at least he was giving me the attention I needed, that I wasn't getting at home. I was also feeling, "What's good for the goose is good for the gander." I felt single in every way and was enjoying it.

I would tell Jack and our friends, whenever we would get together, that I was planning to move to Florida sometime in the near future. Our friends would just look at us both, wondering why. We never talked about it to our friends, but I know they realized something was up. I don't think Jack ever thought I was serious about it.

My daughter was giving us problems during her senior year in high school. I would take her to school and she would go out the backdoor of the school. I was adamant about wanting her to graduate and she promised me that if I purchased her high school ring for her, she would graduate. Needless to say, she did not keep her promise by graduating, but instead ended up having to get her GED, instead.

She would get up in the mornings and pretend to go to work. One day, I called her place of work and they said she no longer was working there and hadn't been working for a while. I was so upset with her for lying to me!

I called Paul, back in North Carolina, and tried to talk with him about her behavior and he would say, "This is not what Pam has told me." I said, "Who do you believe, Pam or me?" He said he would believe Pam. I put the phone down and did not speak to him for many, many years. How could he not believe I was telling him the truth, and why did he think I would be calling him about her if it wasn't true?

Things began to get more difficult between Pam and me, too, and it became unbearable for me with all the stress. She would stay gone all night with her friends and sometimes she would come home late and sometimes not at all. Her personality changed so drastically that I finally told her to get out of the house, that I could not live in "her" world any longer. She moved out to live with one of her friends.

From the very beginning, even when we were dating, Jack had a tongue that could rip your heart out when he was angry. I suppose you could call it mental abuse. He knew how to upset me and he took advantage of that. Even our friends and family members would come to visit and see it.

One evening when he was home, we had an argument. In his anger, he said, "I know who I can call if I need someone to talk to." I said, "Oh yeah? Well, go for it." He picked up the phone and went into the bedroom and called a girl he had confided in previously. She had told him that if he needed someone to talk to, she would be available. After he got off the phone, I walked into the bedroom and said, "You have finally done it this time!" I picked up my purse and walked out the door; leaving both cars in the driveway. I walked up our street to my girlfriend's home. It was almost midnight and I was so angry and I couldn't care less. She lived about four blocks from our house. I had made up my mind that I was leaving him, for good! I suppose I had been thinking of it for a while, and thinking that our relationship had to end, that it could not keep going on this way. We both seemed to be miserable.

A man driving by stopped and asked me if I needed a ride and I said, "No!" He continued, saying he was a nice man and trying to help and was I sure I didn't want a ride. I responded, "What part of no do you not understand?" He sped away.

CHAPTER 24

IT WAS NOVEMBER, 1989 and the morning after I walked out, my girlfriend drove me back over to my home, after I knew that Jack had left for work. I picked up my clothing, pictures, and personal items and threw them in large garbage bags and into the car. I took all of my and my children's photos off the hallway wall and piled them into the car, then headed back to her home.

In the meantime, I called my daughter, Pam, to meet me. She was eighteen years old and had been living outside the home for a while. I discussed my affair with her (which was to be regretted) and felt she was old enough that she should know and understand what was going on in my mind. She seemed to understand why I wanted to leave and go to Florida and we hugged and said our good-byes.

I boxed up all my belongings and took them down to UPS and had them shipped to my sister Alice's home in Florida. (She and Leonard had divorced and she was living with her new boyfriend.) I purchased my ticket and left for Florida the next morning.

It was storming when I left Redding, and while seated on the plane, I was just numb. It was a small commuter plane from Redding to San Francisco. As I was sitting in my seat, I was thinking that if it would only crash it would take away all of this misery. It was a sad time, to be leaving all my friends, my daughter, and John and Dan.

When I arrived in Orlando, Florida, Alice picked me up at the airport and we drove to their condo on Merritt Island. It was a beautiful November day and their condo overlooked the Indian River.

I loved Florida and planned to stay there the rest of my life!

Everything was beautiful, warm, and tropical. My sister and I had a wonderful time, shopping, beachcombing, and attending aerobic classes together. Her boyfriend was a car salesman and he kept an eye out for me to get a good deal on a car. He found one; a little sports car. I was so happy to finally have a way to get around without having to depend on them.

I began sending out resumes; sending around sixty to seventy before it was over. I hadn't heard back from any of them, so I contacted Kelly Girl Services for temporary work. I went to work at a couple of part time jobs in the area; the Cape Canaveral Space Center, and a diet and exercise center.

We were looking for a condo for me and things were going pretty well. We did find one but I wanted to wait until I found a full-time job, before making a commitment.

I was reading a book about Howard Hughes's life and couldn't put it down. It was so interesting to me to know that a man could be so intelligent but be so weird in other ways; letting his life get so messed up with his fear of germs! He did have a very interesting life, though. It made me realize that no matter how much money you had you could still have a miserable life.

I began receiving flowers from Jack. One week, I received a bouquet from him every single day. He would write letters asking me to please come home. I would never respond to him because I had no intention of getting back with him. I was looking forward to my new life.

In March, I received a phone call from my girlfriend (the one who helped me when I left) in Redding, telling me that she was really worried about Jack. She said she had seen him and he looked terrible. He had lost weight and was looking ill. This worried me a lot because I didn't want anything to happen to him!

I would go to bed at night praying that God would help him get over our split and be able to go on with his life. Again, I asked God, "So be your will. Here I am, again, asking for your will to be done." I may have strayed away from my faith, at times, but my faith never left me.

One particular night, I was praying and fell asleep while I was praying. When I awoke in the middle of the night, I could hardly wait until it was 9 a.m. on the West Coast. I had such a strong feeling to call Jack.

When I finally got to call him in the morning, I asked him if he wanted to come to visit me. He quickly replied, "Yes!" I surprised myself, not to mention my sister, who was flabbergasted to find out what I had done. I just told her that I felt like God was leading me. It was such a strong feeling that I couldn't deny it.

Jack flew out to Florida the very next day. I drove to meet him at the Tampa airport. He had once worked in Tampa, so he knew a neat motel to stay that night. We talked way up into the night. He kept telling me that if I went back home we would both move back to Florida. He appeared different and it felt like his attitude had changed, completely. He seemed to be back to the same Jack I had once known.

The next day, we drove over to Merritt Island and he wanted me to tell him everything that had happened. (The affair was his main concern.) I told him all about it and how long it had gone on. He became so upset; I became upset, too.

He admitted that he had known about my affair for a while. He said my daughter had told him everything that I had told her, previously. I found out she had told him everything, even some that wasn't true. I thought, well, things can't get any worse! Now, everything was out in the open and I felt relieved that it was.

We, both talked a lot, cried a lot, and realized that we had put too much time and effort into our marriage to let it all go. He told me he had always felt I was his soul mate (I felt the same about him) and that he still felt that way. Now, we had decided to make every effort to save our marriage.

He promised that we would move back to Florida as soon as we could get things worked out at home and that none of this would ever be discussed again. I believed him and we began our drive back to California. We took our time travelling across country; it gave us time to talk and rekindle our relationship.

CHAPTER 25

WE WENT THROUGH some major thunder storms driving back and my little car would spin out in the strong winds and high waters from the rain. Jack was accustomed to driving nice cars; he never liked my little car and said that we would trade it in when we got back home.

Things felt good to be home with John and Dan and to have our home back. Things seemed normal again. I felt that this was the best thing that could have ever happened for our marriage; to take a break from each other.

On one particular trip to Sunriver, Oregon, we were returning home and the roads were icy. We had the jeep in 4-wheel drive on Highway 97. At one point it looked like the roads were melting and we turned off the 4-wheel drive. At that moment, a transfer truck was passing another truck and was coming head on into us. Jack tried to get off the road but hit ice and the car sped around and around, and going right under the wheels of the big rig. Finally, I screamed, "Let it go!" He took his hands off the steering wheel and we spun right off the road into a snow bank. We sat there stunned and being thankful that we weren't killed. The truck driver never even stopped! We were quiet all the rest of the way home and when we told the children about it, they didn't seem to realize how close we had come to dying.

My daughter, Paula, decided to come back to California from North Carolina with her boyfriend and her daughter. (She had married and had a little girl. She was separated from her husband and she had a new boyfriend.) They drove across country and it was good to see her again and have her back home with us.

She and her daughter stayed with us until we found an apartment in an upstairs unit in a two-story home. I helped her decorate it and spent a lot of time with them when I wasn't working.

Our lives had changed for the good and things seemed wonderful for us. Jack got a local position in Palo Cedro as an appraiser and was able to stay home full time. The children seemed to settle down and things couldn't have been better.

Paula's ex-husband wanted to come to see their daughter and he drove out to California from North Carolina and stayed for a while with them. We thought they might get back together, but, as it worked out, he had other intentions.

One day, Paula and Pam had gone to the store and he took little Megan, their daughter, and left for North Carolina. We believe he had intentions of kidnapping her prior to his arrival. When we realized what had happened, we called the police to report a kidnapping and we were told that we couldn't do anything about it because it was her dad, and we did not have a court order. If we wanted to try to get her back we would have to go to North Carolina to do so, since that is where he lived!

This began the long road of Paula having to go to court. She had to travel back and forth to North Carolina every time there was a hearing, and she also had to have an attorney in North Carolina. Paul helped her find an attorney out there, but he didn't do anything to help, it seemed. Eventually, Paula and her ex-husband were awarded joint custody and Megan was returned to California to live with Paula. We were happy to have her back with us, again.

Jack had always wanted to live in the Northwest, so he began looking for work there. Eventually, he found a contractor position in Chehalis, Washington. Even though it was a temporary position, we sold our home and packed up to move to the Northwest. It must have been God's will for us not to go to Florida, because it appeared everything was falling into place.

We rented a new, 800-square-foot condo in Olympia; wondering how we would get all our furniture in such a small space. We managed to put it all together, except for one large sofa chair that was donated to Goodwill.

We lived in Olympia for nine months while he was working on his job in Chehalis. He would travel from Olympia to Chehalis on a daily basis. I got a full time position with Kelly Girl Services, interviewing and assigning clients to part-time positions. During this time, I was also going to real estate classes in the evenings for a Washington Real Estate License.

We looked at property in Olympia and came close to purchasing a home in that area. However, we never felt comfortable living that far north. We would also travel to the Oregon coast and to Bend, Oregon, looking at homes. After an intense search, we decided to buy a condo at Salishan in Gleneden Beach, Oregon. It was a three-story duplex townhouse with two-bedrooms, two and a half baths, a fireplace in the living room, and wall-to-wall windows, overlooking a deck, creek and trails. It had two decks and a detached one-car garage.

Salishan is an upscale residential resort located on the Oregon Coast, along Highway 101, between Lincoln City and Depoe Bay. It offers an upscale resort lodge with an eighteen-hole golf course, indoor tennis courts, an Olympic-sized swimming pool, and an exercise room. It was built by John Grey, who also built the Sunriver resort outside of Bend, Oregon. He also developed John's Landing in Portland, Oregon. Salishan is one of the most upscale resorts on the West Coast.

Jack had visited this area, previously, and had played tennis at the resort. He had always liked the area and had spoken highly of it. We felt lucky to have the opportunity to live in Salishan. We also liked Sunriver and it was hard trying to decide between the two areas.

While he was still on his job in Chehalis, we moved our belongings from Olympia to our condo we had purchased in Salishan. We stayed at the Red Lion Motor Inn in Kelso, Washington, until he finished his job. This motel was located half way between Chehalis and Salishan. This would allow us to go home on the weekends. We did this for almost three months until we could move full time to the Oregon Coast.

Jack began looking for contract work, again, because there weren't many positions available on the coast. He found a position with Cellular One located in Bend, Oregon. This would allow him to work closer to home and all his travelling would be in the Northwest. He also got me a job, (through a friend) with Northwest Pipeline in working with mapping the pipeline down through the I-5 corridor. I had to go to all courthouses and look up property owners addresses along the pipeline route, from Olympia, Washington to Eugene, Oregon. This was a temporary position, also, but good pay.

We had always loved the Hilton Head area and had visited the island several times. We purchased a nice Villa in Shipyard Plantation, close by the beach. This would give us a place to go visit and we could rent it out as extra income. It was a lovely two-bedroom upstairs unit overlooking the pool. We spent a few vacations there and had Jack's son, Dan, and his wife (Jessica) and children, along with my son, Rick, and my sisters, Jo and Alice Faye, come to visit us.

(Alice Faye, Me, and Jo)

(Alice Faye and Jo at Hilton Head)

(Shipyard clubhouse)

(Dan, Jessica, and Lindsay Leigh)

(Me with Lindsay Leigh at Hilton Head)

(Jack, Jo and Alice Faye at Hilton Head)

Jack had always wanted to have a yacht and live on it. This was his dream and he was forever going down to the harbor, watching the yachts sail in and out. We had such a good time visiting Hilton Head and always thought we would live there full time, someday.

CHAPTER 26

IN 1991, I walked into a real estate office in Lincoln City, looking for a secretarial position. As I was visiting with them, they advised me to get my license to become a realtor. They told me I had what it takes to make a good realtor. I told them I had taken classes in Olympia for Washington's license, but I was told I would have to take another course for Oregon's license. I signed up with them to take an Oregon course; they offered it in their office in Lincoln City.

I took the course and passed my testing in Salem and then had to decide what office I wanted to work in. This office had already set up a desk for me and the managers took Jack and me out to dinner. However, I did not really feel comfortable in the cubical they had assigned me and felt I should look around a bit before making a decision.

The realtor who had helped us find our condo in Salishan called me to ask me to come back into their office for an interview. (She had heard that I had taken the real estate course.) Her office was located in the Salishan Marketplace and she thought it would be perfect for me. I could drive down the hill to my office each day; I could even walk, if needed. After my interview, I was hired and began working as a realtor, two days later.

We were getting settled in Salishan, making new friends and going to functions. Jack became president of our condo association and I became secretary. We really felt good living there and were very happy.

I was doing very well in real estate, and being in a high-end market, it became quite easy for me to pick up leads and customers. Jack was doing well in his business and we felt we had made a good decision moving to Oregon.

(Daddy prior to his death)

In 1992, I received a call from Alice, saying that we were losing daddy. He was dying but his wish was to hang on until we could all be there. Alice Faye told him everyone was there (even though I wasn't there) and it was okay to go ahead. He passed away in the hospital with colon cancer. All my siblings were by his side; I was unable to attend his funeral. Now, we were really feeling like orphans, with both our parents gone.

Now that we had twelve grandchildren, Jack and I decided to open a mutual fund for each grandchild. This would be of help to them with their college or whatever they needed at the age of eighteen years. At Christmas and their birthdays, we would contribute to their fund, instead of giving toys and such.

Being in real estate, I was always looking for a larger home for us in Salishan. I told Jack about a home that was on the market. It wasn't as large as we thought we wanted, but it was a very well-built house and was designed and built by an architect from the Portland area. It was a two-story house, with two bedrooms, two and a half baths, and a galley kitchen. It also offered four covered decks and a detached two-car garage. It overlooked the Salishan Lodge with a distant ocean view. We moved from our condo into our new home in 1994.

Sometimes I would sell one house two or three times in the same area. I became friends with many of my clients and they would locate here from all over the world. The Salishan area is a unique market in which to be selling homes.

Also, in 1994, the owner of our real estate company planned to sell out and close down our office. There were seventeen real estate agents working there. We decided that all the agents would go in together to purchase the company. We put all necessary items together for the purchase in one weekend: hiring an attorney, an accountant, and even giving the company its new name.

I continued with my real estate training and received my GRI (Greater Residential Institute) and CRS (Certified Residential Specialist) designations. My title changed from realtor to broker/owner of our company.

Our company did well, however throughout the years the owners/stockholders narrowed down to just five of us left. All the other owners had either moved or passed away. We continued running the company, always wondering who the next owner would be to leave the company. We had 10 agents working with us.

Our company's location was envied by other real estate companies in that we were located right inside the Salishan Resort. The office location was the best in the area. We did open another office in the Lincoln City area, but when the recession hit, we closed the doors and pulled back into the Salishan office.

Jack and I had joined the Salishan Lodge Tennis Club and exercise facilities. It was convenient for us; like having our own restaurant and lounge and indoor tennis facilities.

(Me with my friend, Ann)   *(Jack with high school friend, Bob)*

We enjoyed playing tennis with our friends and neighbors at the tennis facility. We would go down to the exercise facility on the weekends when he would be at home, and as often as time allowed.

Jack continued to work for the next nine years, travelling around Oregon. I felt comfortable living in a gated area and safe while he was away. Slowly, his business began to slow down so much that he decided to retire in 2001.

Then, the worst day ever in our history happened! On September 11, 2001, the Twin Towers in New York were hit by al-Qaeda terrorists! Everyone remembers where they were on that sad day. We were still asleep and my daughter, Pam, called to tell us to get up and turn the TV on! From that moment on, our lives would be changed forever.

(The Twin Towers in New York)

Hijacked United Airlines Flight 175 flies toward the World Trade Center twin towers shortly before slamming into the south tower, left, as the north tower burns following an earlier attack by a hijacked airliner.

American Airlines Flight 11 was a domestic passenger flight that was hijacked by five al-Qaeda members on September 11, 2001, as part of the 9/11 attacks. They deliberately crashed it into the north tower of the World Trade Center in New York City, killing all ninety-two people aboard and an unknown number in the building's impact zone. The aircraft involved, a Boeing 767-223ER, was flying American Airlines' daily scheduled morning transcontinental service from Logan International Airport, in Boston, Massachusetts, to Los Angeles International Airport, in Los Angeles, California. The aircraft crashed into the north tower of the World Trade Center at 08:46:40 a.m. local time.

United Airlines Flight 175 was a scheduled domestic passenger flight that was hijacked by five al-Qaeda terrorists on September 11, 2001, as part of the 9/11 attacks. They deliberately crashed it into the south tower of the World Trade Center in New York City, killing all sixty-five people aboard and an unconfirmed number in the building's impact zone. The aircraft involved, a Boeing 767–222, was flying United Airlines' daily scheduled morning transcontinental service from Logan International Airport, in Boston, Massachusetts, to Los Angeles International Airport, in Los Angeles, California. The aircraft crashed into tower two (the south tower) of the World Trade Center at 09:03 a.m.

At 9:50 a.m., an hour after the first crash, the first World Trade Center tower collapsed in smoke and rubble.

United Airlines Flight 93 was a domestic scheduled passenger flight that was hijacked by al-Qaeda on September 11, 2001, as part of the 9/11 attacks. It crashed into a field near the Diamond T. Mine in Stonycreek Township, Pennsylvania, near Indian Lake and Shanksville, during an attempt by some of the passengers to regain control, killing all forty-four people aboard including the four hijackers. No one on the ground was injured. The aircraft involved, a Boeing 757–222, was flying United Airlines' daily scheduled morning domestic flight from Newark International Airport in New Jersey to San Francisco International Airport in California. It is believed that the hijackers were intending to crash the plane into either the White House or the Capitol Building.

A third plane, American Airlines Flight 77 crashed into the Pentagon (the headquarters of the United States Department of Defense, leading to a partial collapse in its western side.

(The Pentagon in Washington DC)

-Total Death Toll from These Attacks-

The 9/11 attacks resulted in 2,996 immediate (attack time) deaths: 2,977 victims and the 19 hijackers. A total of 372 people with non-U.S. citizenship (excluding the 19 perpetrators) perished in the attacks, representing just over 12 percent of the total. The immediate deaths include 246 victims on the four planes (from which there were no survivors), 2,606 in New York City in the World Trade Center and on the ground, and 125 at the Pentagon. About 292 people were killed at street level by burning debris and falling bodies of those who had jumped or fallen from the World Trade Center's windows. All the deaths in the attacks were civilians, except for 55 military personnel killed at the Pentagon.

The United States responded to the attacks by launching the War on Terror and invading Afghanistan to depose the Taliban, which had harbored al-Qaeda. Many countries strengthened their anti-terrorism legislation and expanded law enforcement powers. Having evaded capture for years, bin Laden was located and killed by US Navy Seals in May, 2011 and his body was dumped in the ocean.

(Osama bin Laden)

It was hard to continue with our normal life. However, I continued working hard in real estate. One day, while I was holding an open house in another gated area called Little Whale Cove, Jack came with me to the open house. He sat there looking and listening to all the realtors' comments, and when the Open House was over, he looked at me and said, "You know, I think this could be our home. I can see us living here." I looked at him and said, "We can't buy this home; I have it listed! I put the price on it! What will the owners think when I tell them that we want to purchase it?" He said, "We will work it out."

I spoke with my broker, telling her that we wanted to purchase the home I had listed and I asked how I could go about it. She told me that I needed to approach the owners and explain to them that since I wanted to purchase it, they had the right to cancel me as their agent and get another realtor to represent them.

Jack and I setup an appointment with the owners and went over to their home and sat down with them and explained that we loved their home and wanted to purchase it. I gave them the option of assigning another realtor. They told me that they trusted me and that was the reason they had hired me as their realtor in the first place. We began working out the details.

Of course we had to pay full price (since I had put the market price on it). All papers were signed and our offer went into escrow on February 11, 2004.

The sellers had requested a ninety-day closing to give them time to find another home. We closed escrow on May 10, 2004. In the meantime, I had also sold the house we lived in and they would close consecutively on the same day.

(Our new home in Little Whale Cove)

This home was much larger than the 1,900-square-foot home we had in Salishan. It was approximately 4,000 square feet and offered wrap-a-round decking, three bedrooms, three baths, a floor- to-ceiling fireplace, a sunken living room, and a catwalk upstairs (an open hallway balcony). The master suite was huge with a fireplace, refrigerator and a balcony. There was an oversized bathroom with a Jacuzzi, sauna, and bidet. It also offered a large walk-in, built-in closet.

We regretted having to leave Salishan, but we had planned to remain here for only five years and then move to the sunshine and the tropics. We were such sunshine people!

CHAPTER 27

I SIGNED UP to be on a doubles/mixed doubles tennis team and Jack signed up with a 3.0 singles/doubles team. We became very active with Salishan's tennis program and began playing in tournaments again. Jack would travel with me to other cities for tournaments and I would go watch him play.

Things were going well and we were very happy with our new home in Little Whale Cove and we still had a connection with Salishan. We were still invited to join our Salishan friends with their dinners, functions, etc. Even though we were making friends in Little Whale Cove, we still stayed in touch.

In July, 2005, while we were having dinner (after Jack had been playing in a tennis tournament at Salishan), Jack jumped up and ran to the sink, spitting up his dinner. We had no idea what was happening and we were quite concerned. He said he felt like his food wasn't going down and it seemed to be backing up into his throat. Because it was during the weekend, we had to wait to call the doctor the following Monday morning.

He admitted to me that he had been having problems in the past with swallowing his food and that he had acid reflux quite frequently and felt that it was the problem. I had noticed that he had been taking a lot of antacids, but Jack was one not to complain of his aches and pains.

After getting an appointment with the doctor, the doctor suggested that Jack have an endoscopy performed. The next day he was admitted to the hospital for the procedure. I waited in the lounge until they called to say it was completed.

When I walked in to see him in the recovery room, he still had his cap on and I said to him, jokingly, "You look like a little old lady." He said, "Have you spoken to the doctor yet?" I said, "No, I haven't seen or spoken to anyone." Jack said, "They think I have CANCER!" My heart sank and all I could do was to just sit and look at him. I asked to see the doctor and they said he had already left. I was so upset that he had not discussed the prognosis with me and had told Jack while he was still sedated!

The following day, I called the doctor's office and complained telling them that I thought that he had been very unprofessional in the way he had handled it. I told his nurse that the doctor had very little bedside manners! All she could do was to apologize. Jack was referred to a specialist in Corvallis, Oregon.

On July 25, 2005, after seeing the specialist, the prognosis was correct that it was esophageal cancer. We were both devastated. That was another day our lives would be changed! Jack always said that July was the worst month for him because that was the month bad things always seemed to happen to him. He was referring to his daughter's death, and it was the same month he had been diagnosed with thyroid cancer after leaving the navy and had his thyroid taken out. But it had gone into remission many years ago.

We tried to figure out what to do next. Of course, we wanted to get the best care, so we decided to go to Scottsdale, Arizona to the Mayo Clinic. We had faith that they could give us the best treatment possible. We arranged to fly down to Phoenix, rent a car, and rent an apartment, and we planned to stay as long as it took for the surgery to remove the cancer.

I informed my real estate company what was going on and they supported whatever we had decided to do. We left town with high hopes that the Mayo Clinic would be able to help. Esophageal Cancer was not as common, then, as it is today and we knew very little about it.

We rented an apartment, close to the clinic. We had to go every-day for tests—too many to mention. Finally, the date was set for his surgery.

Jack's son Dan and his wife, Jessica, and their two children came down to Scottsdale to be with us during the operation. They would stay as long as we needed them.

During his surgery, we had left to go to lunch and I held a beeper so that after the surgery they could beep us to let us know when it was completed.

We had no sooner sat down at the table to eat lunch when the beeper went off. We immediately knew something had to be drastically wrong! Worrying, we hurried back to the hospital and were met by an attendant, who told us to go into a room where the doctor would come to talk with us. We were thinking the very worst—that he may not have made it through surgery!

The doctor entered the room and he had a look of sorrow on his face. He told us that when they went in to begin the surgery, they did a test on his lungs to see if the cancer had moved into his lungs. It had indeed entered his lungs. The doctor said that he made the decision not to remove his esophagus (which is what they had planned to do). He did not want to put him through all the burden of the surgery, knowing that it had spread already into his lungs. Again, we all sat there, feeling numb, and stared at each other, crying. We knew the doctor was saying that nothing could help him at this point. The doctor was very compassionate and caring.

Even though they had not performed the surgery that had been planned, he still had a six-inch incision through his ribs. It took time for him to heal prior to returning home again. In the meantime, Dan and his family returned home while Jack and I remained in Scottsdale. We remained there for one month. We did a lot of talking, trying to plan what we could do to help prolong his life. We decided that we would begin chemotherapy as soon as possible, with the possibility of radiation, if needed. I was trying every kind of herbs that we heard might help, too.

Being that my daughter, Paula, was living in the Bend area, we decided to begin chemo in Bend. We would stay with her so we would not have to travel from the Oregon coast to Bend for treatment and we would drive home on the weekends.

This routine worked for a while, until winter and bad weather set in; then, it became difficult to get over the Cascade Mountains because of the ice and snow. Eventually, we decided to go back to the coast and have the chemo treatments at Lincoln City Memorial Hospital. This turned out to be a better arrangement because now we could be at home and I could continue working. I would go sit with him during his chemo treatments that lasted for seven hours at each interval. It became a routine for the two of us.

From the very first treatment of chemo, his health began failing. He would never be the same again. The doctor who was handling his chemo told him that he should do things that he had always wanted to do and that it would depend on him as to what type of "quality" of life he would lead from here on. Jack replied, "My quality of life went out the window on July 25, 2005, when I got the news that I had cancer." He gave up from the very beginning.

You can never know the pain one feels watching a loved one die, until you've been there—the days I would have to go to work and leave him sitting on the sofa, having to tell him not to get up for anything, being afraid he would fall. I would wonder if he would even be alive when I returned from work. I felt I had to leave for work because I was a co-owner and things at work needed my attention—and needless to say, our bills needed to get paid.

I would try to talk with him about happier times and even told him what a great life we'd had together and he would just look at me, saying, "Don't you understand? I am dying." All I could think of to respond with was, "We are all dying. You may just be going before us." It is really hard trying to make conversation with a loved one when they have given up and leaving you. I have never seen a book on how to talk to a person when they are dying. Jack would just sit with his head in his hands. I would ask him what he was thinking and he would just say, "You don't want to know!" Now, he really was a man of very few words.

On April 26, 2006, Jo, Alice, and my son, Rick, flew out from the East Coast to be with me. It was wonderful having them there for comfort and to help out with him for a while. During their visit, all our children and their families came up to the Oregon Coast, and for the first time in many, many years we were all together. Jack would say, "Well, I guess I am dying with everyone here."

He was not supposed to have alcohol, but my sister, Alice, got him to drink wine for the first time since his illness. He was like a changed man. He said he was dying that he might as well go out happy. She had him up dancing and it was so good to see him smiling and being happy for the first time in almost a year!

(Alice and Jack)

It was Easter and the little ones had an Easter egg hunt on our deck (in between the sleet and rain). Many photos were taken of the event and time seemed to go by way too fast until everyone was leaving to return home.

When things settled down again, we returned to the old routine of me going to work, leaving him sitting on the sofa, trying to eat the food I would leave for him. He was able to go to the restroom, however, we had stairs, and I told him not to even attempt to go up the stairs. When I would return home from work, he would still be sitting there where I had left him, watching TV, and would not have taken one bite of his food.

He was going down fast. As May, 2006, approached, Jack had become much worse. Hospice came to visit, with the advice of his doctor, but after we talked with them they agreed that he was not ready for hospice to step in—neither was I. We were still holding out for a miracle to happen!

He said he wanted to sign up for a medical "trial" procedure in Portland, Oregon. If it didn't help him, maybe he could help someone else with esophageal cancer, and since the disease was just beginning to become an epidemic (as told to us by the doctor) maybe he could help someone else or maybe it would work on him!

We made an appointment in Portland at Providence Cancer Center for an interview. I remember arriving for our scheduled appointment and he could hardly make it from the car into the building due to being so weak. After his interview, he was told that they couldn't accept him for the medical trial because he was on blood thinners. He was so disappointed, and that was the final straw! All his hopes (if he had any) had vanished for living or helping beat this terrible disease.

He became more and more bedridden. I requested that a minister come (from hospice) to speak with him and try to help him and try to console him. Jack's family's religion was Mormon, but Jack never seemed to practice it. As a matter of fact, he would sometimes say he didn't believe in God. He would ask how God could cause so much sadness for him, by letting his daughter die, losing his job, divorce, cancer, etc.

Since I was reared in a Southern Baptist orphanage and had always had faith that things could always be worse and that things would get better, God willing. I always try to think positive—sometimes too much I suppose; it might have led people to think I didn't care. I feel that is the only way to live: day-by-day.

The pastor sat down and talked with him for quite a while and he seemed to listen to him. But, when Jack began to roll his eyes at me, I said, "Pastor, he doesn't believe there is a God." The pastor said, "I know it's hard for us to believe there is a God when we see sadness all around us, but there is a greater being above us all and Christianity tells us it is God." He held his hand and said a prayer. Jack said, "Why is he allowing me to die? I have too much more life to live." The pastor said, "We are all dying, sooner or later." I felt good to hear him saying that because I had told him the same thing, previously.

I had already made funeral arrangements in Redding, California, for Jack, and informed him that I had purchased a plot close by his daughter and his mom and dad. I asked him if this made him feel any better and he said, "No, it doesn't make me feel any better." I thought it would help him knowing where he would be laid to rest and that he would be returned to Redding. I had always joked with him when he would say he wanted to go back to Redding. I would respond with, "The only way you will ever get back to Redding is in a box." He would just smile because he knew we would never move back there.

On Memorial Weekend, Jack's son Dan and his wife and children came up for a visit for the holiday. My daughter Pam and her husband came by to see him, too.

By this time, Jack was really failing, getting weaker and weaker. He was still sleeping in the upstairs bedroom (yes, he was still able to climb the stairs, slowly). He just didn't want to go downstairs and have to get out of his bed. Again, it was great having his son there and taking some of the load off of me. Jack was always happy to see his grandchildren, Lindsay and Colby! He loved those little guys! He would sit on the sofa and play with them.

(Lindsay Leigh)   *(Colby)*

(Colby with Grandpa)

Several days after Dan and his family returned home, my daughter, Paula, came over from Bend to stay with me and help me take care of Jack. She was a CNA (Certified Nursing Assistant) and felt she would be helpful to me. She was a Godsend, particularly at that time.

I called hospice and told them that Jack had quit eating his food and drinks and asked for their help. He had lost so much weight that he was down to 139 pounds.

They were wonderful about coming in and even bringing a bed for him downstairs. He did not want to go down the stairs to the bed that was put in the office by hospice. I called Jack's brother, Gary, to come over and help me get him down the stairs into the other bed. When Gary finally insisted that he go downstairs, he let him help him down. But instead of getting into the bed, he wanted to sit in the living room in his favorite chair. It seemed so good to see him sitting there watching TV, and not having to be in bed. He sat there with us for a couple of hours that evening.

I made a cot for me to sleep on in his room so he wouldn't be alone. During the night he would sit up every once in a while to check to make sure I was in the room with him. I would say, "I'm still here." I had to always reassure him that I was still there.

I knew his time on earth was limited and Paula and I would stay by his side all hours of the day. I would read to him from his favorite novel, *Blue Horizon,* by Wilbur Smith, pages 347 through 362. That's the page he had gotten to while he was able to read.

Paula helped me lift him to go to the potty. He still insisted on getting up to go; he wouldn't use the bed pan. All I could think was that he must have been so embarrassed to have someone else have to help him into the bathroom! He was in no frame of mind to think or say anything, though.

His mouth was drying out and we had to keep wiping his mouth with moist swabs, trying to get the dried up saliva off his teeth and he wasn't taking in any water. He would cough so hard, at times, and I called hospice to come to check on him. She came over and checked him and then made a call back to hospice to give an update. Paula and I knew he was going. His arms and legs had begun turning purple. She left and told us to keep doing what we were doing: giving him morphine and keeping his mouth moist.

Jack's brother, Gary, and his wife, Dee Dee, lived close by and I called them to say that I felt Jack was leaving us. They came over and spent the afternoon with him and did not leave until evening.

Later that evening, around 9:15 p.m., he began to cough intensely and had very hard time breathing. I became so exhausted and upset; Paula held his hand while I called hospice, saying, "What am I supposed to do, just stand here and watch him smother to death!" She said to me, "Just give him more morphine." She said if he kept fighting it, for me to tell him, "It will be okay to go on over." I went back into the room and we gave him another dose of morphine.

When he began coughing intensely again, I told him, "Jack, it will be okay; go ahead and take your daughter's hand or your mother's hand and go with them. 'You are just tormenting yourself by trying to hang on." Jack opened his eyes wide and gave me a stare that I still live with. His eyes were as blue as I had ever seen them. He then closed his eyes and went to sleep again. I held his hand for awhile until I was thirsty and called Paula to come hold his hand while I went to get a glass of water. Just as I had gotten into the kitchen to get the water, Paula called me and said, "Mom, I think he is gone."

Hospice had already directed me not to become upset if he chooses to go while I am out of the room. She said that sometimes they didn't want their loved ones around when they passed on, and that's exactly what he did.

He was gone. I called hospice to tell them he was gone and I also called Gary and Dee Dee to tell them. Gary and Dee Dee came right over and a hospice nurse came over to clean him up, along with the bedding. He was pronounced dead at 9:30 p.m., June 14, 2006.

We all just sit there in silence, waiting for the mortuary to come for him. They arrived about forty-five minutes later and carried him out in a bag. It was pouring down rain outside.

I had already arranged for him to be delivered back to Redding, California, which was a seven-hour drive. The hearse carried his body all the way down I-5 to Redding from Lincoln City, Oregon.

On June 20, 2006, his military funeral was held in Redding and when the "taps" were played I couldn't hold back the tears any longer (I was on tranquilizers). It was good to see some of our old tennis buddies from years back at his funeral. Of course, they were upset to see him, saying, "We would not have recognized him had we not known it was him." He had lost so much weight and looked so drawn.

Even though the funeral home had tried to dress him up with makeup, if I had it to go over again I would not have held an open casket, knowing how upset it would make him for anyone to see him like that. He was a very vain man with his looks.

(Jack's gravesite in Redding, California)

After returning home from the funeral, my son, Rick, came out to Oregon to spend some time with me. I enjoyed him so much, especially since everyone had left and I was trying to get things back to normal again. He helped me with yard work, being that was my favorite pastime and therapy.

My cat, Chancey, had gotten out of the house and had been missing for days. I was devastated, to say the least. My husband was gone, and now my cat! We have a lot of wild animals around the neighborhood in Little Whale Cove, with a lot of vegetation, and I just knew something was going to get him. I would lay awake at night thinking a cougar or coyote had gotten to him.

Rick told me to put Chancey's litter box out on the deck, that cats could smell their litter box a mile away. We were watching TV and low and behold, we looked up and there stood Chancey, looking in the sliding door at us after 3 days! I was so happy to see him again!

Rick returned to North Carolina and Chancey and I were there at home all alone. We went through a few terrible storms in the evening. The lights would go out and I would sit there with Chancey via candlelight, crying and talking to him, thinking about everything that had happened.

Several days later, I was cat sitting Gary and Dee Dee's cat, Shadow. I was out on the deck, staining the deck table and chairs, when all of a sudden, I saw a flash go by. I thought maybe one of the cats had gotten out! I ran inside to check on them, and when I got inside, the ceiling fan (twenty-two feet high up on the ceiling) was running. I heard a noise in the office where Jack had been sleeping prior to his death. When I got in the room, that fan was running full speed. I had not turned either of the fans on. Actually, I had never used them before!

I felt so much energy in the house and I got so excited because I felt like Jack had spiritually been in the house! He loved this house so much. I began talking to him, saying, "I know it's you and I know you are here!" I began to tear up and I was so excited to actually be feeling his presence. I really do believe he had been there and that the flash I saw on the deck was him finally leaving our home. Maybe my Granny Jordan's tales were really coming true for me.

When I told Gary about the phenomenon that had taken place, he just said, "Only Jack could have done something like that." Now, I truly believe that after death your loved ones can visit you. I know what I saw and felt! Gary and I thought a lot alike as far as spiritual beings.

One of the most miraculous things we all experienced was that in October of 2006, Jack's son, Dan, and his wife, Jessica, found out that she was pregnant! They had already had two children and felt they had completed their family; she had been on birth control pills to make certain of it.

The baby would be due on June 14, 2007—the same day of Jack's passing, the following year! We were all surprised to learn of this.

A baby boy named "Carson" was born to Dan and Jessica on Dan's mother's birthday of June 12 instead of June 14, 2007. He was named after one of Jack's favorite football players at USC, Carson Palmer. We refer to little Carson as our miracle baby!

CHAPTER 28

I REALIZED THAT having to attend to Jack I had missed the busiest and best year in real estate on the Oregon Coast in many years. The market was beginning to slow down and the economy was doing the same. For about four months I tried to get back into work and tried to keep busy to keep my mind off of things. But, the Oregon Coast is so laid back, and there isn't a whole lot to do for someone who is single and alone. I was also realizing it wasn't for me any longer.

I called my sister, Jo, who lived in Delaware, and planned a trip to visit with her and try to determine what I wanted to do with the rest of my life and where I wanted to live, work, etc. I went to Delaware and spent a couple of weeks and had pretty much decided I might move there. I returned home, thinking that I may move, but being a co-owner of the real estate company I felt I had an obligation to the company. So, I continued trying to get back into real estate. However, since I had visited her in August and had planned another trip to see her in October, my business was slowing down and the co-owners were beginning to wonder about my future plans.

In September of 2006, one of my single girlfriends at work tried to convince me to get on a dating site on the internet. Other friends tried to set me up with dates. I did go to dinner one evening with a nice gentleman, but his name was Jerry and I just couldn't see myself spending time with someone having the same name as mine. I know this may sound superficial, but that's the way I felt at the time.

I did begin getting more involved with tennis, but all my tennis partners would go home to their families and I would go home, alone. Things were so quiet around my house that, one night, I decided to do what my friend had suggested and checked out a dating Internet site.

Thinking it might be fun, I signed up and enjoyed emailing back and forth with a couple of guys, but nothing developed other than one telephone call, which only lasted a few minutes. The site I had signed up with was not sending me the type of men I had requested. I called the site and told them to cancel my subscription immediately.

A couple of months went by and I called my sister, Jo, again and decided to take another trip to Delaware, still trying to determine what to do with my life. My life still seemed to be in disarray and I couldn't decide what I wanted to do with it.

In the meantime I signed up with another dating site on the Internet, to determine if it was any better than the last one. This time, I expanded my search further toward the valley and closer to larger towns. I felt this would give me a better chance of finding someone.

After one week on this dating site, I met a gentleman from Portland, Oregon. His name was Jim and I was so taken by him after reading his profile. He was such a gentleman and could do anything around the house, such as electrical, plumbing, and building repairs. He was tall—six foot two—and handsome. I felt I had met my "knight in shining armor!" He was the Godsend that I needed.

Jim's profile on the dating site read, in his own words:

"Let me see now—my friends and family would describe me as: a casual gentleman with character and integrity, who is successful, well grounded, easy going, intelligent, decisive, loving, kind, outgoing, fun to be with, moderately active, passionate about the important things in life, assertive, (when appropriate), secure with self, and knows what life has to offer. Accepts challenges easily and is polite, sensitive, compassionate, and understanding.

I would add that: I have high family values, love to laugh and have fun. I enjoy good conversation, most kinds of music, and love romantic weekend getaways, snuggling in front of the fireplace, RV camping, and cruise-ins. My life is active with frequent trips to the gym, hiking, boating, hiking, traveling the beautiful Northwest, back roads and other wonderful destinations, and walking on the beach with my dog,

"Cobey." I also enjoy fine/funky dining, going to the movies, photography, and attending some sporting events. There's a side of me that enjoys the elements of culture, such as museums, theater, and ballet; I can even be taken to an opera without complaining too much. But I also like to relax at home—happy with a fine glass of wine, a fire, and good book, even a video. Occasionally, I tend to immerse myself in "home improvement" projects, as I am very good with my hands. I also have a willingness to try new things and a keen perspective on what really matters. I respect the need for individual space and I am emotionally stable and available. As a Libra, balance is an important factor in my world. My life is fulfilled in many ways with one obvious exception. I am seeking a special friendship, (to start with. . .) bound by mutual acceptance, understanding, and respect. If this description of my world and me is what you're interested in, please write and let's explore the possibilities!"

How could anyone not be interested in a man with these qualities? Not to mention that his photo showed him with beautiful "tennis" legs—one of my passions!

Then when I read what he was looking for in a woman, I felt it described me, totally. "She's passionate about life and the things that are important to her. She's emotionally stable/available, a good communicator, attractive, fun loving, has a good sense of humor, is honest, open, intelligent, spontaneous, energetic, family oriented, independent, with physical health being of high importance. She enjoys romantic candle lit dinners, either at a nice restaurant or cooked by the two of us. She loves affection, having doors opened for her, flowers on special occasions, or for no reason at all. Enjoys outdoor activities, walks hand in hand and is comfortable in an evening dress or her favorite jeans. She is self-confident and looks for the positive in her surroundings."

In October of 2006, I had planned to take the "red eye," that left Portland at 10:25 p.m. for my visit to my sister, Jo, in Delaware, and Jim said, "I live in Portland, so maybe we should meet at the airport prior to you leaving?" We planned to meet at the airport restaurant for dinner. I waited in the background looking for him, and when I saw him, I pretended to walk past without noticing him. He looked at me and said, "I know you." He recognized me by my photo. We both laughed and that broke the ice right away!

After we had a glass of wine and dinner, somehow we got on the subject of kissing. He asked me, "Do you like to kiss?" I looked at him and said, laughingly, "Get your ass over here, and I will show you!" It didn't take him long to slip over into the seat beside me in a booth. Of course, we kissed!

(Our first meeting at the airport in Portland, Oregon)

We sat and talked until it was time for me to board the plane. I didn't want to leave him and he said he didn't want me to go. We asked the waitress to take our photo and this is our first photo made together.

I spent two weeks in Delaware and he called me every evening at 9 p.m., East Coast time, which was 6 p.m., West Coast time. We would talk for hours at a time. We were really getting to know each other well.

When I arrived back in Portland, he met me at the motel where I had left my car during my trip. We went to breakfast and then we drove over to his home prior to my leaving for the coast. I was able to see where he lives and meet his dog, Cobey. Then, I was on my way back home to the Oregon coast, which is a two and one-half hour drive. All the way home I was thinking that I had met the right guy for me!

CHAPTER 29

I FELT WE had, both, found a perfect match on this dating site. For a year and a half, I continued to live on the Oregon coast and Jim would come over to visit and I would go over to Portland to visit him in Portland, whenever my work allowed it.

It took me a while to tell Gary and Dee Dee that I had met someone new. I didn't know how they would react and I really cared what they would say. However, after I told them about Jim and they had the opportunity to meet him, they liked him and we would go to dinner together quite often. They felt we were lucky to have found each other.

One day a man called me to say he and his wife were looking for a house to rent in a nice area and he had gotten word that I had talked about maybe renting my home someday. I had previously contacted a rental agency to check on pricing for rentals should I decide to move out of the area.

I called to tell Jim what the caller had said and he said, "Why don't you just move to Portland and live with me?" After discussing the issue as to how, when, etc., we decided to do it. I called the renters and put together a rental contract, gave my notice at work, packed all my belongings, and me and my cat moved to Portland in one month, February of 2008.

Even though I had given my notice at work, I left my real estate license hanging in the office to be able to get any referrals from the other realtors.

Moving to Portland was a good move in that I did not feel alone anymore and Jim and I got along great. He would tell others how well we got along, and that we never had any arguments.

Jim had been born and reared in Phoenix, Arizona. After his graduation he had attended Phoenix College. After college he worked in semi-conductor manufacturing over 40 years, prior to his early retirement in 2004. At his last job he was responsible for the design and construction of three wafer "state of the art" manufacturing facilities, the latest one being in Hillsboro, Oregon.

He had been a bachelor for twenty-two plus years. He had been married and was divorced with two children, a son and daughter. He had been on dating sites before, so I was a little hesitant, thinking that maybe he had been a bachelor too long and it would be hard for him to live with someone again. Although he had been married previously, he had been living alone for such a long time.

I had visited Puerto Vallarta, Mexico, before and had stayed at a resort called Dreams. I told Jim about it and we decided to plan a trip to Mexico in October of 2008. It was exciting since it was our first trip together. What a beautiful time we had. It was like a honeymoon in Heaven! We told our family that we were just "practicing" for our honeymoon!

(Mexico Trip 2008)

I can still smell the aroma of the flowers, the clear blue waters, and feel the soft white sands between my toes. The local people were so friendly and the resort had five restaurants, shows every evening, along with a couple of lovely swimming pools for guests who don't like the ocean's salty water.

Jim showed me a recreational side of life I had never experienced before. We took dune buggy rides, skidoos, the big "yellow banana" ride, and quads. We still talk about that vacation and how much fun it was. This would be the beginning of a lifestyle I had never been accustomed to.

One evening there was a tremendous storm while we were there. It went on all night long, with lightning illuminating our room so bright we had to eventually draw the drapes to be able to sleep. However, it didn't rain one drop; it was a far away dry lightning storm. We did hear the thunder in the distance. Jim said that was the worst storm he had ever seen!

Jim's best friend, Cobey his dog had been with him for ten or more years, became ill and he had to have him put down. It was really hard on Jim and it took a while before we decided to get another dog. In August of 2008 we got an Airedale puppy and named him "Tanner." He has been such a joy to us both. It's amazing how much joy and fun an animal can bring to a family! It has been said that you can never replace an animal that you once loved, but it sure can help you to forget.

Our lives have become complete by him.

(Tanner, our Airedale)

Once, while we were in the vet's office, I was telling the vet about a foul odor coming from Tanner and he said, "It must be his anal sac; it comes from the wide animal in him."(I thought he said anal sex.) I looked at him funny, since I had never heard of it. So, when the vet left the office to get something, I asked Jim, "Do dogs have anal sex?" He looked at me and laughed and called me, "Gracie," (referring to George Burn's wife). The vet heard our conversation outside the door and came in laughing so hard, saying, "I am going have to share this one!" The joke was on me because I was dead serious!

I'm always saying things that make Jim laugh, not really meaning to, however. I have been told by my friends, in the past, that I should write a book, listing all of my "aphorisms."

Jim's mother had been a beautician and had owned a beauty salon in Phoenix. His dad had driven a linen truck that delivered clean towels to the salon and that's where they met. They were married for fifty years. I never had the opportunity to meet them, but I feel like I knew them by listening to Jim talk about them. He was lucky to have had such a normal life.

We came from such different backgrounds. He had a more normal life with his family; he had a mom and dad, a sister and brother, went to church, and never had to worry about having food on the table. Jim was the middle child, too, having both an older sister and a younger brother.

Jim proposed marriage to me in December of 2008 by saying, "I guess we should go look at rings." He said he wanted to show our children what his intentions were and that he was serious about his and my future together. We already knew that we would be together for life, anyway.

In the summer of 2009, we planned an engagement get-together, bringing in all my children and his children at Sunriver, Oregon. We rented a large house and it was wonderful having everyone together.

There was quite a crowd at the gathering: my son, Rick and his girlfriend and son; Jack's sons, John Jr. and his wife and two sons and Dan and his wife and three children; Paula and her husband and three children; Pam and her husband and three children; Jim's son, Jim, Jr. and his wife and three children; and Jim's daughter, Danielle and her husband.

It turned out to be a great time to get all the family together and to introduce the families to each other.

(New Year's Eve)

Months turned into years, and family members and friends asked us when we were going to get married and we would say, "We aren't in any hurry; it will most likely be next year." Each year, that is what we would say. After four years, I was beginning to think that Jim had been single much too long and we would never get married. We would talk about it and then it would be put on the back burner, so to speak.

In June of 2010 I received a telephone call from my sister, Alice, telling me that my dear sister, Jo, has passed away. I felt like I had been hit between the eyes with the news! I cried as hard as I had cried in years, thinking and saying, "Everyone I've ever loved has left me!" Jim didn't know exactly what to do with me, so he called my daughter, Paula, to give her the bad news. She told him not to worry; she would come over right now to be with me.

Paula and I arranged to fly out to Delaware the following day to attend Jo's funeral. It was such a sad time being together with all my brothers and sisters, again, under these circumstances. But, it was a bittersweet time, too.

Jo was like our mother and she was the patriarch of our family. She is truly missed by us all.

We have a family reunion each year in August in North Carolina. She was looking forward to her trip down there and had already begun packing her car for the trip. There was a tremendous void without her presence, but we still managed to go ahead with it. We felt that it was what she would have wanted us to do.

(Pat, Alice, Me, Herman, and Robert [2010])
(If you look closely at this photo, you will see a "face" between Alice Faye and me? We sure felt Jo's presence that day.)

Jim has always been an avid 1930s Hot Rod fan and had always wanted to build a 1934 Ford Coupe. When I first met him, he had a 1934 Ford Coupe in storage. It was a "barn find" and it was so rusty and old! I felt he would never be able to restore a car like that, but he proved me wrong.

(Black Ice)

"Black Ice," as he named it, was in the building stage for six years. It took up most of his time and things would get a little tense around home because he was on such a schedule and timeframe. The coupe was finished in June of 2012. It is a beautiful car and it's his "baby" and his dream. At Black Ice's first show it won first place in its category.

On September 25, 2012, my best friend, Chancey, my cat that had been by my side for thirteen years, became ill and I had to make the decision to put him down. I had never had to do this and it was so hard. I remembered all the times he was with be during my husband's illness and death, and the long dark nights at the beach when the electricity would go out during storms. He brought me so much comfort and solitude. I am still holding onto his ashes and just waiting for the right place to lay them to rest.

(Chancey)

Jim's daughter, Danielle, was married in San Diego, California, on September 13, 2012. We drove down to the San Diego area for their wedding (along with our dog, Tanner). Jim gave Danielle away at the wedding and of course everyone was asking us, "When are you two going to get married?" We would just say, "We are talking about it."

We discussed it and thought December 12, 2012 (12/12/12) would make a good date. At least it would be an easy date to remember!

We arranged to go to Reno, Nevada, to be married. We had always wanted the ceremony to be in the Little White Church, in Hillsboro, Oregon. However, they required months to arrange and we wanted to go ahead with the wedding prior to the New Year.

Jack's son, Dan and his wife and family, Danielle and Shawn (Jim's daughter and new husband), and my daughter, Pam, were at our wedding in Reno. It was a simple but a beautiful wedding and things went well as planned.

(Our wedding 12/12/12)   *(Following the wedding)*

When I first met Jim, he had four cars lined up to complete the restoration on, but he sold two of them. Now he has one in storage and the other one he has built for a client. He has been working on it for two and one half years and it will be completed and delivered in 2014.

Since our wedding, Jim has been working diligently on the 1933 roadster to get it completed. Our life has seemed to come to a halt. We haven't had the opportunity to travel or do the things we have always wanted to do.

(Cruising in Seaside [1933 Roadster])

(1933 Roadster [Completed])

I have spent most of my time, gardening, putting together jigsaw puzzles, reading, and writing this book. Of course, I spent a lot of my time training and raising our little guy, Tanner.

Now Jim is presently co-owner and chief operating officer for a new Internet website known as Carbuff Network.com. It went public in November, 2013, at SEMA, in Las Vegas, NV.

(Jim and me on our First Anniversary [12/12/13])

We are looking forward to our life together. Our future plans are to travel and promote the website and attend cruise-ins around the United States.

(Our first Thanksgiving after our wedding with Dan and Pam's families [2013])

(Our First Christmas with Jim's family [2013])

Our married life is doing well and Jim and I are very happy living in Portland, Oregon. We just returned from a trip in January of 2015 to Cancun, Mexico. Our dream is to stay healthy and continue with our happiness!

Siblings:

-Jo, born 12/26/1938, in Wilson Mills, North Carolina (at home), married Jim Bretti had one child, Cindy. Divorced and married to Carl Madden had two children, Carla and Eric. (Jo passed away June 5, 2010) Her family resides in Selbyville, Delaware.

-Alice Faye, born 4/16/1940, in Wilson Mills, North Carolina (at home), married to Dean Argue had three children, Debbie, Dean, and Billy. Divorced, married Leonard Bentley had one daughter, Andrea.

Divorced and married Jim Hogan (Jim died in 2012). She resides in Kenly, North Carolina and Melbourne, Florida with Leonard Bentley.

-Pat, born 9/12/1941, in Wilson, North Carolina (Wilson Hospital), married Wiley Pegram had three children, Rhonda, Yevonne, and David (Wiley passed away in May, 2013). She resides in Stokesdale, North Carolina.

-Jerrie, born 3/14/1943, in Wilson, North Carolina (Wilson Hospital), married Paul Phillips had three children, Richard, Paula and Pamela. Divorced and married Jack Duckett (Jack passed away 6/14/2006). Married Jim Stewart and they reside in Portland, Oregon.

-Herman, born 10/22/1945, in Raleigh, North Carolina (Rex Hospital), never married, resides in Kenly, North Carolina.

-Robert, born 11/12/1946, in Raleigh, North Carolina (Rex Hospital), married Judy James had two children, Robin and Della. Divorced and married Toni, (Toni passed away in 1990's). Married Rhona, had one son, Clayton. He is now divorced and resides in Stokesdale, North Carolina.

(Family Photos). . .

(Herman, Jerrie, Robert, Alice Faye, Jo, and Pat, homecoming at Mills Home, [2006])

(Pat, Jo, Jerrie, and Alice Faye [2009])   *(Pam, Rick, Me, and Paula)*

(Pat, Alice Faye, Jerrie, Herman, and Robert at family reunion [2013])

(Jack and My children: John, Rick, Paula, Dan and Pam)

(Rick)   *(Paula)*   *(Pamela)*

CPSIA information can be obtained at www.ICGtesting.com
Printed in the USA
BVOW06*1432011115

424520BV00006B/55/P